Five Years on the Appalachian Trail

By Buck Innerebner

Dedication

To my Daughters and my Grandsons.

Something to remember the Old Man by.

Novels by Buck Innerebner

Tales From Wild Cat Canyon

Old Indian Café, Champion, Mi.

The Last Summer

Five Years on the Appalachian Trail

By Buck Innerebner

Cover Design by Buck Innerebner

Published By Wild Cat Canyon Press

ISBN-13:978-1469904269

ISBN-10:1469904268

September 2012

Acknowledgments

Thank you Bernadine Innerebner

Thank you DeWayne Jewson.

Thank you Jami Moran.

Thank you Jim Innerebner

They helped me plow around the stumps.
And there were many of them.

Springer Mountain, Georgia, April Fool's Day, 2007. Rain fell lightly as I took my first steps along this 2,176-mile footpath leading to Mt. Katahdin, Maine. My backpack weighed over 45 pounds, tonight would be my first ever sleeping in a tent. Five years later upon summiting the big mountain up north, I thought myself to be an experienced hiker. This is a short account of that journey. The things I liked as well as the things I did not.

PRELUDE

My first thoughts of hiking the Appalachian Trail came to me several years ago on the trek down from the 11,400-foot marker on Mt. Rainier. It was a failed attempt with my wife's cousin Bobby to summit the 14 thousand foot volcano in western Washington State. My feet were bloody from the rented plastic boots I wore, required equipment that I would need to affix my rented crampons. It was a huge disappointment, for the past eight or ten months our thoughts were channeled in one direction, get ready for this trip, this adventure. We bought equipment that could not be rented, tried to get in shape, talked on the phone, long distance, me in Georgia, Bob in Texas, about standing on top of the greatest mountain in the lower 48. For certain we were not real mountain climbers but this was something, with a little planning, ordinary people could do, hell, Al Gore did it, so our confidence was high. On the way down the mountain that day, I thought of winding up and throwing my ice ax as far as I could, just for the hell of it. Then I remembered they had my credit card number and was sure I would end up paying 150 bucks for a 35-dollar hatchet that I did not even get to use. I hate getting beat but beat we were, the mountain beat us, the weather beat us, and maybe some of us beat ourselves by expecting too much. We were both runners, both played ball and stick games and Bobby even ran a stock car for a while. For the most part winning was expected but today we found out how it was to lose. As thirty of us weary, defeated souls marched in lock step down the mountain, some cold, some hot, all tired, we met a fresh group of highly inspired want-to-be mountaineers heading up the mountain. They looked similar to what our group looked like yesterday. If they only knew what us south bounders knew. If you ever attempt to do something like this find and pay an outfitter to take a group of two or three. It will be worth the extra money and your chances of reaching the top will increase dramatically. With large groups, you are only as fast as the slowest team member is and the cattle mentality makes for a long day. I do not remember the cost of this adventure, a very good selective memory at work, but it was still worth the price of admission. Now I know I am not cut out to be a mountain climber, but I am a slow learner, have been all my life, I had to try it before I would be convinced of it. There are no more serious mountains in my future but I do from time to time have thoughts about Mt. Kilimanjaro. At 19 thousand feet, a non-technical climb requires only a little endurance and stamina and I would suppose a lot more money. I can only envision the "look" I would get from the wife if I brought something like this up between the salad and the turkey on Thanksgiving Day.

After turning in our rented gear, Bobby and I limped across the parking lot to his pick-up truck. Even with our comfortable leather boots, we stepped lightly.

I caught Bobby's eye and told him, "If I ever mention climbing a mountain again, shoot me, and if you don't have a gun, get one, and shoot me."

The 15-foot snow banks surrounding the parking area made us look like dwarfs, and this was the end of May. For the first couple of miles going back to the motel our frame of mind was little grumpy, pissy, I guess you could call it. Then the joking and laughing started, in our early fifty's and trying to act like kids, if the fountain of youth was on that mountain it was not to be found but we realized that the last 24 hour period would be with us forever. Even the person that crosses the finish line dead last will have memories of the event. Closer to the motel the chatter turned to doing something less strenuous, maybe hiking the Appalachian Trail, or the Pacific Crest Trail. That would be fun, the feeling was mutual. "Do you think we will ever grow up?", I asked. "I hope not," he replied.

I believe the recently retired Bobby was 55 or 56 years old at that time. I asked him how it was going and he told me that when he turned 62 and started drawing Social Security he was going to buy a brand-new Lincoln. It sounded like things were going well but I do not know for sure. The next day was the last time I saw or talked to him, he leaving for his home in Texas and me heading east to Georgia. There have been family weddings and funerals, even a reunion, I have attended some and he has attended some but never have we attended together. I am not avoiding him; I doubt he is avoiding me but maybe we both know that it would take very little pressure for us to start checking

9

availability on Delta Airlines up to Seattle. I hope he gets his Lincoln.

Awhile back, I mentioned to a good friend, Gary, that I was thinking about hiking the Appalachian Trail and told him I was looking for a partner. He put on a few pounds since he ran his last marathon but the guy never quit anything he started so I was confident that if he committed to going he would be there at the end. I was a little disheartened when he asked, "What's the Appalachian Trail?"

It is all I thought about for the last year, reading books, checking stuff out on the internet, and I even spent thirty bucks to join the Appalachian Trail Conservancy. How could anyone not know about the finest foot trail in the world? "Well Gary," I took a deep breath. "It's a trail, goes from Georgia to Maine."

"Oh yeah. How far would that be?"

"About 22 hundred miles," I replied.

"Whose truck would we take?"

"Ahhh, no, it's a walking trail. Walk all the way, sleep in a tent at night and cook our food on a little gas stove we would carry with us."

Now it was his turn to breathe deep "Did I mention I been going to a special doctor in Iron Mountain, one of them acupuncturists, for my arthritis, been killing me the last couple years. Doc told me in 20 years or so I could be in a wheelchair."

I had to think a second before responding, "Well gee, I know you're 60 now so in 20 years you could be dead too so maybe a wheelchair might be the better option."

"Yeah but I got a bad back too. You remember when I rode the kid's bike all the way to Ishpeming? I swear part of that seat is still up my butt. Other than that I'd go along, in a heartbeat. No kidding. Well, good seeing you again, see you later."

"Where ya off to? Are you still throwing horseshoes?" I asked, not wanting to give up so easy but knowing it was not going to work.

He turned, "Yep, every Wednesday night, first place in the old timer's league."

I knew I had lost, I wished him the best and, "Well, hope you get better soon."

I got the feeling my old running buddy did not want to spend 40 days walking in the woods with a 40 pound pack on his back, eating macaroni and cheese almost every day for dinner and feeling fortunate to get a shower every five or six days.

My plan was to "section hike" the trail. Forty days or about 500 miles for four consecutive years. The first leg would start at Springer Mountain in northern Georgia, up into The Great Smoky Mountains National Park and end about 40 miles north of Damascus, Virginia.

Enter my Grandson, the football player. Fourteen years old, about five foot ten and 180 pounds. On two occasions while conversing with other people about walking the trail, Justin mentioned that if not for school he would hike with me. I brushed it off as just that, 14 year old talk but then it came up on a third occasion so I asked what his schedule looked like. "I've got the last week in March and the first week of April off." He told me with a rather confident voice, knowing that his old Grandpa would try to make something happen.

Some "thru-hikers," the ones that do the entire trail in one season sometimes will start in mid March to early April but invariably they run into snow and just plain nasty weather once they reach the Smokey's. I intended on leaving around the middle of April, almost assuring me of at least half way decent weather. He wanted to go and I wanted him to go so a deal was made, departure would be the first day of April, "celebrate the fools," I told him, and he could spend the first week with me and his mother would pick him up around the seventh. I hoped that would give us enough time to reach Franklin, North Carolina, about 105 miles from our starting point.

I had already bought a 90-dollar sleeping bag that was good for 30 degrees but leaving two weeks early made me take it back and exchange it for one that was good for 20 degrees and another 30 dollars out of my pocket. It was 150 smackers for my tent, the most expensive pair of boots I have ever owned came in at 170 bucks, my backpack set me back about 150 and I still had a good deal more to buy. It is not as if I have always hiked, or even camped. I have not, this was a first for me and everything I would need was at Dick's Sporting Goods, not out in my garage. I still needed a water filter, hard telling how much for that, and some good rain gear, probably about a hundred dollars. Plus all the little stuff, and there is lots of little stuff, ten bucks here and 20 bucks there and I just knew my budget would not stand the test of my, "need to have," list. This stuff, "Gore-Tex" was killing me. If something made out of nylon costs a hundred dollars, the same thing made out of Gore-Tex would cost 300 dollars. The plan was to come up with a little extra cash but in reality, the Minister of Finance told me she was not parting with another dime. I ended up going to Wal-Mart to get the rest of my gear. I love Wal-Mart, other than Home Depot it is my favorite store but it is probably not a good place to buy hiking gear when you are a rookie and going on a 40 day hike out in the wilderness. I know, it is a well-marked footpath but with me behind the wheel, the parking lot at K-Mart has at times given my wife fits of laughter as I have zero sense of direction. I always try to park in the same place but oh well, if you know what I am talking about I do not have to explain and if you are lucky enough not to know that helpless feeling I doubt I could enlighten you.

It is still a month before Christmas and my plans are starting to firm up. Another running buddy and lifelong friend has expressed interest in joining me on the trail for, "a week or so." Mike was born and raised in the Upper Peninsula of Michigan. Having just announced his retirement from Wells Fargo after 37 years gave me hope that he might stick around for more than, "a week or so." Having played high school sports, basketball, track and cross-country plus city league hockey in his younger years he was now a five-handicap golfer. I was positive that if we hiked three days in the rain and cold and stunk like Billy goats he would still be there on that fourth morning boiling water for coffee. Mike would fit best in the category described as ultra competitive. Definitely the Alpha Dog. I have known him for almost 50 years; we probably drank our first beer and smoked our first cigarette together. We not only learned to play penny ante poker at my Grandpa's house but also learned a little about life.

Enter hiking buddy number three; Tom is a long time friend of my brother Jim, both living in Michigan's eastern Upper Peninsula. Tom has hiked extensively out west and has logged many miles on the Appalachian Trail. I was up there in November, 2006 for the deer-hunting season when Jim introduced us. It was good for me to talk with an experienced hiker. We went to his house and looked at all his gear, I had a hundred questions, he gave me a cat stove and we made fuzzy plans of potentially meeting on the trail the next spring. It was a long shot, me not sure when I would start; he had a trip planned to Russia. We exchanged E-mail addresses and phone numbers. Six months later, we hiked almost 200 miles together.

CHAPTER ONE

APRIL 1, 2007

SPRINGER MOUNTAIN, GEORGIA to ATKINS, VIRGINIA

An Old Dog Learning New Tricks

It was in all probability not a good day for a couple of rookies to start a hike. It was not raining but the falling mist made use of the windshield wipers a must. We left home on that Saturday morning, April 1 at seven A.M. A quick stop at the local Waffle House for breakfast and we were on our way to Springer Mountain, the southern terminus of the Appalachian Trail, or A.T. as it is known. For me it was the conclusion of two years of planning, reading all and any information I could find, spending in excess of a thousand dollars for equipment, and trying to talk unsuspecting people into coming with me. The first to take me up on this little adventure was my 14-year-old Grandson, Justin who just happened to have time off from school. He sat in the back seat amongst piles of hiking gear, a smile on his face that within 24 hours would start to disappear. Taking a Forest Service road to the top of the mountain saved us an 8.8-mile hike on the approach trail from Amicalola Falls State Park Visitors Center. Apparently, the 2000-foot rise in elevation from the visitor's center to the top of the mountain was enough to discourage many other hikers as the parking lot was not full but there were at least 15 vehicles parked along the road.

I know. What is another 8.8 miles when you are planning to walk 500? Well, less than one mile of the approach trail is part of the A. T. and I did not intend to walk almost eight miles that would not count just to get to the start of a hike that would lead me into southern Virginia.

The mist was still falling but it would take much more than a little rain to dampen the spirits of the 12 or 14 other hikers that were gathering at the trailhead. Some were preparing for a walk lasting as little as a week but in most cases, the hikers that leave this early in the year are planning to go all the way, 2,174 miles to Mt. Katahdin, Maine.

Before hoisting our backpacks for the first time, Justin and I attempted to attach our pack covers. Pack covers are nothing more than cheap, ten-dollar pieces of plastic that protects your backpack and its contents from the elements. Later in the trip, I would spend 30 dollars on one that actually worked. After posing for pictures in front of a U.S. Forest Service sign, there was a waiting line, I gave my very understanding wife a kiss, she got a hug from her Grandson and the hike was under way.

The start of the trail is well-maintained, gentle rolling hills. In fact, the hills were rolling mostly downhill. The first 4.1 miles have a negative elevation change of about 1,250 feet. It was the first of many tricks and surprises this great trail would play on me. We hiked on, stopping every 40 to 50 minutes for water and a small snack. After just three hours, I knew my pack was too darn heavy. Forty-three pounds in a backpack walking around the yard at home did not feel quite as daunting as it felt now. My shoulders were killing me but not nearly as much as Justin's back was bothering him. The weather in Georgia for the past two weeks had been un-seasonably warm. With temperatures in the low 80s, the allure of the old swimming hole was un-resistible for 14-year-old boys. In addition, they have no idea that a little sun screen would do wonders to thwart a severe sunburn. Our goal that day was to walk to Hawk Mountain Shelter, a total of about six and a half miles. We made it but were more than ready to stop. As the day played out the skies cleared, the haymaker came out and the rising humidity made things very sticky.

Hawk Mountain Shelter sleeps 12 and was jam-packed when we arrived at 5:30 PM. Justin and I found a reasonably level spot behind the shelter and pitched our tents. After getting water from a source about 300 yards behind our campsite I fired up my "cat" stove and ate the first of what would be excessively too many Ramen Noodle dinners. The cat stove was a homemade gift from Tom Kurtz who would later join me on the trail in Erwin, Tennessee. It consisted of two cat food cans, a small one inside a larger one with several holes punched along the bottom. A small amount of denatured alcohol poured in the bottom rapidly produced enough boiling water for the noodles and coffee. Because of the bear situation in the North Georgia Mountains food hoist cables were available. We used them but I think it was mostly for show as I had two candy bars in my pocket for later that night and I would bet Justin had a snack or two himself. My biggest fear was running out of food, not running into a bear.

By 7 P.M. the first days light on the Appalachian Trail was vanishing into dark, the shelter was full and I counted no less than 20 tents set up around its perimeter. It was reassuring to know we were not in this thing alone.

Sleep came easy but it did not last. I have a mattress at home made out of some space age material that conforms to the shape of my body, gives a little but remains firm, or so the salesperson said it would. Regardless, it is a very comfortable way to spend a night. The same cannot be alleged for the three quarter inch closed cell foam-sleeping pad that I lay on that night. Had I not been extremely tired I doubt I would have slept at all. In the course of that first night, we listened to automatic weapons fire from Army Rangers stationed at nearby Camp Frank D. Merrill. At 5:30 AM sharp, a nearby Hoot Owl started hoot hooting. He was either looking for a long lost love or for breakfast and it took him a full 40 minutes to find it. I would hear a similar sound almost nightly for the next 300 miles of my hike.

I crawled out of my tent at seven the next morning, a little stiff and a little sore but the adrenaline continued to flow and a bit of discomfort was almost welcomed. It was the first time in my life that I slept in a tent and better than that, I could walk all day on the A.T. and sleep in the darn thing again tonight. Justin's first question of the day was, "Papa, did you bring toilet paper?"

I served instant oatmeal and coffee for breakfast, another meal most hikers would quickly grow to dislike. Before getting back on the trail that morning, we went through our backpacks and ditched some of the foolish stuff to lessen our loads. A very bulky set of headphones, a seat cushion, a deck of cards, stuff I thought would be nice to have along, and it would have been nice but I sure as heck was not going to carry them. For the next seven days, I would eliminate at least one item per day from my pack.

The cool morning soon turned warm and then hot. Our goal for the day was a reasonable 7.6 miles to Gooch Mountain Shelter. Justin's back was turning into more of a problem than I could expect a 14 year old to cope with. He advised me earlier in the day that he thought this would be a once in a lifetime experience so I understood he was not having a lot of fun. He did not know how close I was to agreeing with him, this was tougher than I thought it would be. Justin decided it would be best if he left the trail as quickly as arrangements could be made. Fortunately, my cell phone worked and his Dad agreed to pick him up the next day at Woody Gap. We made unhurried but steady progress, resting frequently while drinking plenty of cool mountain spring water and munching on granola bars and trail mix. About two miles from our destination, we had the good fortune to meet Glen. From the Indiana farm county, Glen graduated from Michigan Technological University in the Upper Peninsula of Michigan, just 50 miles from where I grew up. A prospective thru-hiker, he hoped to walk the full 2,000 plus miles to Maine in one summer, Glen's wife and son dropped him off at Springer Mountain the same day Justin and I started. We would stay together, meeting almost daily for the next twenty days.

That evening was spent about the same as the previous night. It took us about an hour to pitch our tents, filter water and prepare dinner. It seemed most hikers then gravitated towards the shelter where there was a fire ring and picnic table. Talk was mostly gear related or about the terrain covered that day or what the maps showed for the next day. It was a 7:30 bedtime and again the rangers and the owls made their nightly sounds along with a very hard rain on our tents.

The sun came up the next morning but refused to shine, it was cool, 40 degrees and the overcast firmament would accompany us for the remainder of the day. After breakfast, we packed up wet tents and hit the trail. It was five miles to Woody Gap; the last four were hiked in a heavy wind pushed rain, our ill-fitting pack covers convinced me to acquire a better one at the first opportunity. As we stepped out of the woods at the road crossing, Justin's Dad was there waiting. A quick hug between Grandfather and Grandson and Justin was in the back seat of a warm vehicle and there I stood, buckets of rain pouring off the brim of my hat with just 20 miles covered and 480 to go.

The trailhead at the Gap provided picnic tables and a privy with a long overhanging roof, which offered a reprieve from Mother Nature's continuing rain. I spread peanut butter on my last bagel and washed it down with warm water. It would be the last bagel I ate or the trail, if you think about it; the darn things are very heavy. Walker, another thru-hiker from Tennessee soon joined me in what would soon become a group of ten or 12 hikers all moving at about the same speed that I would spend time with on the trail or around a campfire at night. Walker was his real name not a trail name but I guess it fit the bill. He was thirty something, balding and very thin. Soft spoken with a laid-back demeanor and very friendly. In addition, he was patient, where I used an alcohol stove to cook my food he burned small twigs the size of pencils in a tin can to heat his rations. It seemed to take forever just to get the darn thing started. Not a situation I could have handled with my McDonalds, hurry, hurry, hurry, mentality.

Back on the trail, I crossed my first river but it was not as you see on the cover of National Geographic where they struggle through fast moving rapids with backpacks held high over their heads. I stepped on two evenly spaced stones and had it not been raining the bottom of my boots would have stayed dry. The rain continued, at times heavy and at times, showing a break in the cloud cover, giving me hope it might be coming to a halt. Walking in the rain, I have read somewhere that it is good for the soul but it was not doing a thing for my $170 pair of, "guaranteed to keep your feet dry" boots. As I, and everyone else on the trail would soon discover, Gore Tex and all the other high-tech fabrics that have gone into boot and clothing development over the past decade does not work as stated in the glossy colored advertisements you see in Backpacker Magazine. I started thinking about all the planning that went into this trip, at least ten books read, research on the internet and visiting with other hikers. Talking to salespeople in the stores, some wanted to help but other just wanted a sale. After just over 30 miles, I realized that all the prep work I did was of some value but the trail itself was by far the best teacher. It was not going to change, having been here over 80 years it was up to the individual hiker to adapt.

At 5:30 that afternoon, despite the rain I was feeling good about myself as on just my third day on the trail I hiked 12.5 miles. I walked into Wood's Hole Shelter thinking that maybe there would be a brass band waiting for me but of course, all I found was eight other cold and wet but amazingly cheerful hikers. Wood's Hole Shelter, built in 1998 and named in honor of Tillie and Roy Wood, operators of the Woods Hole Hostel near Pearisburg, Virginia. As I was soon to discover several of the shelters, spaced between six to 12 miles apart carried the names of people that have made significant contributions to the trail. The majority of them slept between 8 and 14 on uncovered wood floors surrounded by three walls and open at the front. For the most part the shelters had a water supply within a half-mile and some as close as 100 feet. Most had a privy and some had bear cables, heavy wire run between two trees with several pulleys that allowed us to lift our food bags out of a bears reach at night. At shelters without the cable set up or, when as frequently happened, camping between shelters we were left to finding a suitable tree with a horizontal limb about twenty feet off the ground. I will confess that on some nights I just said "the heck with it" and stored my food bag in my tent thinking that if a bear attacked I would beat the blessed hell out of him with my trekking poles. I am originally from the Upper Peninsula Michigan and know how big some of those bears can get, I am thankful I did not get to set my defense tactics into play.

I spent my third night on the trail in the shelter, no one likes to set up a tent in the rain, or worse yet, pack one up in the morning. The shelter built for seven would that night sleep 10. Turning someone away on a cold rainy night does not happen; it is an unwritten rule of the trail. That evening we strung rope back and forth across the rafters to hang wet clothes. Each and every one of us cooked some sort of pasta for dinner, the staple of any long distance hiker, with cookies or trail mix for dessert, all washed down with either filtered or treated water. It was that evening I was bestowed the "trail name" of "Noah." Not much of a talker when around people I am not familiar with I sat and listened to a conversation between a young missionary, just back from two years in a far away land I can no longer remember the name of and a young Jewish atheist from New York who also happened to be a vegetarian. My total years on this earth were more than their combined ages but I never heard such a balanced discussion on evaluation verses intelligent design as I did that night. I listen to more talk radio than I should so I am familiar with different points of view. Both were very respectful, never interrupting but always coming back with another point in a level tone of voice, similar to that of Garrison Keller, so if you were not interested a person could very well have drifted off to sleep. Trail names are as old as the trail itself, given from one hiker to the next to somewhat reflect either a personality or a physical characteristic. That night when asked if I was a thru hiker I responded to "Mousetrap Mike," that, "No, I'm only here for 40 days." "And 40 nights I would presume," added the young missionary, "and you shall now be known as Noah." So there it was, I was Noah. At that point, I had to ask, "Is the story of Noah and the Ark a true story?"

"Probably not a factual description," offered the missionary.

Mousetrap Mike picked up his trail name on the basis that he set eight mousetraps every night in the shelters where he stayed. It was not without controversy as some hikers thought the two-legged hiker animals were infringing on the home of the mice. Those convictions soon went away, generally after only one night in a shelter, as all of them, without exception were lousy with the furry little critters.

The morning came early as with that many hikers confined to such a small area sleep did not come easy and when it did, lasted only a short time. The clothes we hung to dry last night were just as wet this morning but our spirits were high as the day looked to be a good one. After cooking oatmeal and coffee, I set my cat stove on the ground to cool and within five seconds stepped on it with my size 12 boot.

It was only my fourth day on the trail but after yesterday, over 12 miles and baptized under mostly rainy conditions I was feeling good about the whole thing. My virginity was gone, I survived the rain, my body was starting to smell and within the next two miles I would climb Blood Mountain, so named after a battle between the Creek and Cherokee nations that left the mountainside running red with blood. It was also a good feeling to know that after another four miles I would be at Neels Gap, U.S. 19 and 129, the home of the Walasi-Yi Center, a full service outfitter, where I could purchase a new cook stove and wash clothes and take a shower. The stove cost 90 bucks, the shower and washing machine ran another five, and I spent the remaining five bucks from a hundred dollar bill on candy bars and a hot dog that I should have passed up. It is a great place in a great location, only 30 miles from Springer Mountain. A small number of would-be thru-hikers end their quest here.

I hiked out of the Walasi-Yi Center with a young man of Korean heritage. Jae was a 30-year-old

25

downsized computer guy from Chicago with intentions of going all the way to Maine. His given name would quickly give way for the reason that if you are hiking the A.T. and your rain jacket is yellow, and your backpack is yellow you will without end be known as Mello Yellow, shortly after shortened to Mello. We would hike together for the next 20 days.

I spent the night at Low Gap Shelter, 14 miles that day and feeling good other than my right hip was telling me something was wrong, or at least different. I must be getting used to the sleeping pad as I am now sleeping ten hours a night. The next morning after walking for an hour or so, I came across the "James Boys," as they would be known as we progressed up the trail. They were presently breaking camp, having pitched their tent just a short distance from the trail. Though not related both of their first names were James. I took my pack off and visited a short while; again, two more hikers I would see often in the coming weeks. As I left their campsite, James, one of them, was nonchalantly rolling a joint, something I would observe them doing rather frequently as we hiked north. At that time, I was taking two Aleve every morning and two more at night plus a multi vitamin and a horse pill that contained Glucosamine and Chondroitin. On my Aleve bottle I noticed a warning in very small print that said something like, "continued heavy use of this product could result in an increase in the chance of heart attack or stroke." I bet the James Boy's had no such warning on their bag of Happy Hay.

An hour later, I met a group of southbound Boy

Scouts, ten in all I counted as they marched past. The two leaders were perhaps 35 years of age and they all looked like they had more business being out here than I did. For their hike in the wilderness, they would no doubt receive some sort of badge or at least a certificate. I noticed I was starting to smell again, it was the only badge I would earn, the badge of honor of the long distance hiker. Personal hygiene on the trail boiled down to an occasional splash of cold mountain spring water in the face, brushing your teeth in the morning if it's not raining and all importantly, do a real good job wiping your butt.

I stopped at the Blue Mountain Shelter for lunch, peanut butter on crackers and a peanut butter granola bar. It seemed like peanut butter was one of the staples on the trail and I would continue to eat great quantities of the stuff as my journey continued. Each shelter has a logbook used by hikers to leave messages for friends coming behind them or in most cases just to reflect on the day's happenings. One of the entries dated March 25 in this particular book read as follows.

"Remember kids, any pain you may be experiencing is just weakness leaving your body so suck it up and hike."

It was signed, "Loan Wolf." It sounded to me like something Vince Lombardi might have told his football team back in the 60's and in all probability would have had some effect. Probably not so much now.

After a 20-minute rest it was back on the trail, now my other hip hurt and my shoulders were not happy campers. I kept adjusting my pack, and there are more possible adjustments on these things than there is on the space shuttle. Nothing seemed to work, my pack was too heavy and I was too scrawny. The words, "suck it up and hike" came back to me and I was starting to like the taste of warm water. I was becoming a hiker. My objective for the day would be only 10 miles but it would include a thousand foot climb from Unicoi Gap to the crest of Rocky Mountain. As younger hikers streamed past me on this uphill, I admit to being a little envious but also proud that some of them acknowledged my being there. There was not a shelter at the apex though the Trail Guide I carried advised me I would find a campsite. It was a great day for hiking but not necessarily a great day to climb mountains. I am not saying ice axes and ropes, and technical climbing methods, just a thousand foot elevation rise over the course of 1.3 miles on a footpath littered with rocks and roots. It seemed to me that it was straight up. When I eventually reached the summit the gentlest of winds greeted me along with some of the finest, by that I mean level campsites that I had yet seen on the trail. Moreover, they were all mine, I could take my pick, I was there alone, it was pushing 6:30, a time when most hikers were at wherever they planned on being. I pitched my tent on the highest point with the door facing south to take advantage of what I thought was a splendid little breeze. Within five hours I would deeply regret this.

About 30 minutes before the day turned to night one more backpacker struggled to the top of Rocky

Mountain. I first met Leonard, newly retired and from Annapolis at a rest spot maybe three days back. We chatted briefly as he set up his tent, he made a quick dinner and we used a common line to hang our food bags. As what was now my routine at 7:30 I was in my tent and more than likely sleeping before 7:45. All was fine until I heard the initial heavy raindrops beating the walls of my tent at around mid-night. Occasional thunder in the distance was of some concern but the wind, at first a fixed blow soon turned into explosions of wind, rain and fire. The lightning came on fast; this actually gave me a little peace of mind as I figured the storm was moving fast and would quickly be gone. It was moving fast but it was a colossal thunderstorm. At times, the sidewalls of my tent were almost touching and I was somehow in between them. The lightning so horrific and so frequent there were five-second stretches I could see perfectly, everything in my tent. To say the least I was terrified. Would I be one of the few people to die on the A.T.? Would I make the 6-o-clock news? Not without a fight. I crawled out of my sleeping bag and got dressed, including my rain gear and boots. My headlamp was handy but it took a minute to find my cell phone. What was I thinking? Most of the time it did not work anyway, it sure was not going to work tonight, but I was ready. If the tent stakes came up and the walls collapsed around me I would crawl out of the darn thing and walk down the mountain. "I'll come back in the morning and pick up what's left," I thought. The electrical storm lasted for another hour and the wind and rain for half an hour after that. About 3 A.M. I fell back to sleep, still fully dressed but only to have a nightmare that a bear was clutching my leg and pulling me out of the tent. I remember thinking, "Well, I should do something about this." About that time I woke up and did not get much more sleep. When the darkness of that night gave way to the much anticipated rays of early morning light, I crawled out of my tent to survey the situation. I have to give credit here to the tent maker. I remained completely dry in a Eureka, Zeus 2EX0. As I lowered my food bag the next morning, I realized that bears were the least of my worries last night.

Leonard was not so lucky, twice during the storm his rain fly twisted around in such a manner that rain was blowing into the tent so twice he was outside making repairs. We talked briefly that morning, he told me after the second time his tent failed he thought of crawling in with me. I told him, "Leonard, if you would have stuck your head inside my tent last night it would have been all yours because I most certainly would have had a heart attack." We laughed a bit, I surmised the situation as I saw it, "It was a hell of night." Leonard, a veteran hiker and one that had his sights set on Maine saw it another way, "Just part of the trip," he said. I saw him only twice after that, once on the trail, where we posed for a picture, and the last time at the Fontana Village Resort where we were both taking a day off and waiting for a snowstorm in the Great Smoky Mountains to blow itself out. I heard later on that Leonard developed a case of gout and his quest of the A.T. was in danger of ending. I certainly hope not, the guy deserves to be a thru-hiker.

Back on the trail I hiked 12 miles to Deep Gap Shelter, it was only 3:30 but after last night, I was ready for a good night's sleep. Tomorrow I would hike less than four miles to Dicks Creek Gap where my wife Sandy would pick me up. Mike, a long time friend from Michigan would then join me on the trail for what we thought would be two weeks. I was looking forward to some restaurant food and a night in a warm bed. I had three toenails that were black, two very small blisters that were of no concern, my left heel hurt, my shoulders and back still hurt but not as much as before so over all things were going well. The night turned cold but thankfully stayed dry. My water bottles contained slush the next morning but I was still able drink it. As I walked out to the road where I would be picked up I tried to assess my first five days on the trail. It was physically harder than expected, the changes in elevation were demanding, up and down, up and down, UUDs someone called them, useless ups and downs. The other hikers were superb, very willing to share advice or a word of encouragement. Sandy picked me up 10 minutes after I got to Dicks Creek Gap. We drove back to Helen, Georgia where she already made reservations at a motel.

Mike was also a first time hiker. We ran marathons and 10-K road races together when we were younger, and a little kayaking just recently but were both new to this game. When I first talked to him about this, he told me it was one of my least crazy ideas. He had all his equipment laid out on the bed and it is not

31

that he had a great deal of stuff; it is that he had too little room to put it. His backpack was a corporate gift he received in Alaska several years earlier. As I looked at it last fall, I told him it might not work but he wanted to try it. It did not work. From Helen we drove back to the Walasi-Yi Center at Neels Gap where he was expertly relieved of $200 and fitted with a great pack.

We were back on the trail mid-morning the next day. About 200 yards in Mike stopped to adjust his new backpack and remove price tags from his other gear. After a quick 500-foot climb, he told me where he kept his heart medication, just in case. It never got above 40 degrees and after seven miles; we pitched our tents in an area with a good water source. Most of the streams we acquired water from appeared as fresh and clear as anything you would find anywhere and in a pinch, I would have no problem drinking it without the benefit of filtering. Its Friday today and for the occasion I opened a can of sardines for supper, talk about smell, if we do not have bears in camp tonight we never will.

The night got extremely cold. We did not know it at the time but all of North Georgia experienced record low temperatures. I woke up at 2:30 to pee only to find a half inch of snow on the ground, and strong winds. Already wearing all my clothing, I added my rain gear and crawled back into my bag. I could not fall back to sleep, I was cold. At 4 A.M. I hollered over to Mike, "Are you awake?"

"Hell," came an immediate response. "I haven't been to sleep yet."

We agreed to break camp; hiking would be the

only way to stay warm. It was a three-dog night and all we had were three season tents and sleeping bags rated at 20 degrees. All our water bottles froze solid. The wind was steady and cold but the trail had been there for 80 years, we knew it would lead us to the road. We had four days of food in our packs and if we had to, we could have built a fire. With headlamps, it took us almost three hours to reach Muskrat Creek Shelter where we found Ghost, a thru-hiker from Massachusetts. The man was as cold as one can get and still be alive. Having set his tent up in the shelter, burning his cook stove and with the help of a space blanket he managed to make it through the night. We stayed long enough to eat a few granola bars and I made a visit to the privy. I could not believe what I saw, a metal toilet seat. Ten degrees and I am going to sit on a metal toilet seat? Not a chance, I found a tree.

The shelter is four miles from United States Forest Service road 71 at Deep Gap. As we left the shelter heading north, all three of us were hoping to catch a ride into Franklin, N.C. The terrain was somewhat flat but it seemed to take an eternity to hit that seldom-used side road. We knew that it would afford almost no possibility of a ride into town but what a surprise upon stepping out of the woods, Trail Angels. Back in the 60's the Lovin' Spoonful sang, "Do You Believe in Magic." My answer then was an explicit "no." A good song but I did not believe in magic then and 35 years later after taking my Grandson to see the world famous Doug Henning my feelings were reconfirmed but on this day I would become a true believer in magic. Trail Angels are just common folks doing uncommon deeds. It is called Trail Magic what they provide. More often than not, they are hikers themselves and have a desire to return something to the trail in response to their own good fortune when they were the ones putting in the hard miles. I heard and read about things akin to this but this group came across as Super Trail Angels. They set up three large tents, had a fire going with tarps hung between the trees to block the wind and I do not know how many stoves were cooking hotdogs, hamburgers, brats, and hard telling what else. This was the day before Easter. Easter Sunday they would be here also, cooking omelets and making sandwiches, any kind you wanted on homemade bread. It was the sixteenth year in a row they have done this, Cook, Tarheel, Raven, Repete, and crew; I cannot express how happy you made us hikers that cold Easter weekend of 2007.

After filling up on hot chocolate and good food Mike and I hitched a ride to Franklin, N.C. where we spent the night at a forty-dollar motel right across the road from Shoney's and an ice cream place; hog heaven! Mike and I were not alone. The prediction of continued record low temperatures caused an exodus of hikers off the trail. Early the next morning we hitched a ride back to Deep Gap. Despite eating breakfast at Shoney's we ate again at the trailhead. There were about 20 hikers there at that time; approximately ten of them spent the night in the woods around the campfire. It was noon before we wobbled back onto the trail, the air was frosty but our bellies were full, it was good to be hiking again.

I have noticed numerous exceptionally large oak trees that have fallen over the years to Mother Nature's horrific windstorms. Some were diseased but others were very much in their prime, solid specimens. Logging is not permitted along the trail. Some would think what a waste of furniture grade lumber but others would be fine with it knowing the fallen tree will make a wonderful home for the squirrels over the next 80 years. The chestnut trees that once made up a quarter of the forest in this area back at the turn of the century are no more. Giant oaks and very tall, straight tu ip poplars now seemed to dominate the landscape thus far, and rhododendrons. At times, they formed a canopy over the trail for hundreds of feet, giving you the sense of walking in a tunnel.

Shortly after a southbound day hiker advised us of fresh snow in the Smokies, a concern to us, as they were only four or five days up the trail. It was another cold night in our tents at Betty Creek Gap. Tree Whisperer and the James Boys were also there. To save weight and room the thought of carrying a pillow does not come into play. Generally, I used extra clothing in a stuff bag, or even rain gear balled up for that purpose but when the temperatures drop below freezing there are no extra clothes for such a luxury. At night, everything you have in your pack goes on your body, leaving for a very flat headrest. The majority of us are out here with three-season equipment and not geared up for freezing weather conditions. My sleeping bag, rated for 20 degrees keeps me alive but not comfortable.

Cold again in the morning, 18 degrees, great incentive to get moving plus the climb up Albert Mountain would make it a tough day. We passed the 100-mile marker from Springer, for me it was 400 to go. That afternoon it was a bus ride from Winding Stair Gap back into Franklin and a room at the Sapphire Inn, a hostel owned and operated by Ronnie Havens. Ronnie is "The Man" in this town; he will pick you up and drop you off anywhere any time, even at a competitor's motel. According to the person behind the reservations desk, this is all scheduled but it seemed no one knew for sure what the schedule was. When a van pulled up you got in it, eventually you got to where you wanted to go. If Ronnie were to run for governor of the state of North Carolina and hikers could vote I believe he would be a credible candidate.

Back on the trail the next morning, many hikers are leaving Franklin as the weather is starting to improve. A good many of them slack packing, the controversial practice of taking a shuttle out of town 15 or 20 miles up the trail and then walking back, carrying only a day pack and water and spending another night in town. The A.T. is marked every few hundred yards with a white 2X6 inch blaze, mostly on trees. There are also blue blazes, marking side trails to water sources, shelters or at times a shorter and easer path around a mountain. Then there are yellow blazes, when a hiker comes to a road and he knows the trail will cross this road again he will walk the shoulder of the road, following the yellow centerline until he reconnects with the trail. I have no problem with any of this; there are no hard fast rules. The saying on the trail is, "hike your own hike." If you are a thru-hiker and make it to that mountain in Maine there will be neither brass band waiting for you nor a government official standing there presenting you a certificate of achievement. For the record, in my first 535 miles I slack packed only two miles.

I have noticed a good mix of age groups on the trail but mostly young guys in their 20s. We old gray beards made up about ten to 15 percent. There were a few interesting characters on the trail and on April 11 we met two of them. The first at Cold Spring Shelter, Eagle, a retired Marine Gunnery Sergeant was south bound. I do not remember what his destination was but in 2006, he did a yo-yo, hiking north to Maine and promptly turning around and walking back to Georgia. He seemed very at ease with the simplicity of the trail, treating it as a home that may not have existed elsewhere. He carried only one water bottle and his pack weighed less than 20 pounds. At that time, mine was over 40. Probably a little less than six feet tall, his frame was flagpole thin and I would guess he weighed no more than 135 pounds. Very willing to engage in conversation he informed us of his stay at the "NOC" Nantahala Outdoor Center, the night before, our goal for this evening. He told us the private rooms do not have TVs. and when he complained, they told him he should be enjoying nature, not watching TV. His response was that when he was on the trail, he would take pleasure in nature but when in town he wanted

Home Box Office. We all had a good chuckle, put our packs on and moved down the trail.

Six miles down the path at Wesser Bald Shelter it was time for another break before pushing on to the NOC for the night. There sat Bubba wrapped up in his sleeping bag, not moving and not greeting us as we removed our packs. He had "stuff" hanging all over the shelter; it looked like he had been ridden hard and put away wet. Mike and I started eating a snack and tried to make small talk with the guy. There was no response at first but after a few minutes, he asked us, "What do you men do for a living?"

Before either of us could answer he offered, "I'm a scientist and I've found a cure for criminal behavior."

"No kidding," was all I could think to say. He went on to tell us of 56 people that he cured from his hometown. I like to joke around as much as anyone does so I asked him if he could make a living doing this sort of work.

"Oh yes, I've had a special on PBS."

I am starting to think the guy might not be joking but I had to ask, "So how does it work?"

He went on for ten minutes explaining pheromones. I could not remember exactly what his definition was, I am not good with big words and he was using plenty of them so I looked it up first chance I had. This is what it said, "A chemical substance that is usually produced by an animal and serves especially as a stimulus to other individuals of the same species for one or more behavioral responses."

Bubba's premise was that if he took chewing gum, the sugarless kind as it left no residue and rubbed it on a mothers forehead after being chewed and then transferred the gum to a troubled child's forehead the offspring would then start acting in a more behaved way. Or something close to that as I was starting to get a little nervous, I had my pack on and wished him well, Mike was still talking to him, trying to find out his real name, it was B. Nicolas. I have since done a Google search and found nothing.

We reached the NOC late that afternoon after 17 miles of tough up and down hiking, probably too much too soon. Our bodies were beat but tonight with the help of real food, a shower and sleeping in a real bed our enthusiasm for the trail would be restored. Eagle was right, no TVs in the rooms but we were sleeping by 8 PM so who cared.

After an early breakfast it was off to the outfitters; Mike bought a new tent, replacing one he thought too small. I bought a new pack cover and a bag of Fig Newton's. Back on the trail, after a night in a real bed I thought it would be easy hiking but it is like something new hurts every day. I suppose it is my body's way of making me forget about what hurt yesterday. Expecting rain again tonight and a temperature drop to 30 degrees, we hope it does not snow. A break with the weather would be just what the doctor ordered, the days are nice but the nights are beating us up, hard to sleep with all your clothes and boots on and still not comfortable. It was 25 degrees the next morning but there was no precipitation of any kind so for that we were grateful. I fired up the stove to cook and Mike asked what was on the menu for breakfast. "Omelets," I told him, "ham and cheese" and then I started heating water for yet another batch of oatmeal. Oatmeal, it seemed my food bag was full of it so I did a quick inventory, sure enough; I probably had enough Quaker Instant Oatmeal to carry me to Pennsylvania. But I was not going to Pennsylvania. My plan was to make southern Virginia. I opened four of the individual packets and dumped them on the ground for the birds and squirrels, there; I just cut five ounces off my pack weight. Did I ever feel good about that.

It was very overcast so we hit the trail with full rain gear and pack covers on. The sky soon cleared and the temperatures begin to rise, within an hour the rain gear came off and it was shorts and tee shirts the rest of the day. It was an easy hitch of two miles into Fontana Village Resort, getting there just before noon. After renting a room and taking showers, we found the restaurant and ate lunch with Tree Whisperer. Tomorrow would be a milestone, it would mark our entry into the Great Smoky Mountains, or so the plan was. The elevation at Fontana Village is 1,800 feet, and there was snow on the ground the next morning. Most of the Smokies are at 5,000 feet and at times goes over 6,000. The Weather Channel forecast for the Smokies included sustained winds of 20 to 30 miles per hour with gusts reaching 60 miles per hour. It was an easy decision and it was a no go. It would by my first zero day, trail talk for doing no miles, a rest day. I bought an "Asheville Citizen-Times," watched the NASCAR race on

TV and ate huge amounts of junk food. Most of the crew I hiked with the past 17 days was there, Walker, Tree Whisperer, Mellow Yellow, K&T Express, the James Boys, 501, Leonard, and more, some I would not see again.

The following morning, with the sky clearing a local shuttle driver delivered us to the Fontana Dam, our starting point heading into the park. The Smokies belong to the government; it is a national park so naturally there would be forms to fill out, permits to obtain, back country camp permits and so forth. It seems day hikers could reserve a spot in the shelters but thru-hikers could not. The shelters are approximately 15 miles apart. It made me wonder what high-level over paid bureaucrat came up with such a lame brain idea. Up to that point, it was first come, first serve and it worked just fine.

It was a short walk across the dam, the highest in the eastern United States and into the woods. By 10:30 AM, the trail was covered with an inch of melting snow. We met a man and woman coming south that spent the night in the mountains. They told us of darn near freezing to death, with much snow and winds reaching 80 miles an hour. After they passed I told Mike, "Yeah, 80 miles an hour, wait till they have a few beers and it will be 110 miles an hour." We enjoyed a little chuckle and moved on; not knowing they were right on the money. It was not a good night to be camping in the Smokies.

After hiking in about six miles, Mike's leg started to give up the ghost. He injured it three days earlier but

41

hoped the zero day in Fontana would be enough time for it to heal. Not so, he pulled up both pant legs and clearly, his right leg was a third as big as the left. It was a no brainier, six miles back to Fontana or 34 miles north to the next road crossing. We shook hands, Mike went south, I north. Mike was only planning to go three more days anyway as our wives were to pick us up at Newfound Gap where we would spend another zero day in Cherokee, N.C.

I pushed on, soon the snow started to melt, the trail turned into a small river, my 170-dollar boots kept my feet dry for about an hour. I made it to Russell Field Shelter for the night. It was packed, like sardines in a can, sleeping bags serving as the mustard sauce. Sleep was elusive.

As I hiked out of the shelter the next morning the blustery weather continued along with two inches of frozen snow and ice on the trail, it made for tough walking. My left leg was killing me and I did not know why, it was fine yesterday. I start to worry, will it end my hike? This was my nineteenth day on the trail; it seemed we were becoming a procession of the walking wounded. Countless minuscule things to wear a body down. Knees seem to be the main cause of discomfort followed by blisters and other foot problems. We are not made, I am thinking, to carry 40 pounds on our backs up and down these mountains. Most hikers are able to work through the negligible injuries but in some cases, it turns into a ticket off the trail. The spirit of the A. T. has by now materialized in my head. It appears to be, hike when you want, rest when you want and eat

42

and sleep when you want but the trail will have the final word on everything. Pay attention to the maps and pay particular attention to your body. Be content with what the trail gives you. Some days it may not give you much.

After the first mile from the shelter, I started to encounter blow-downs across the trail. Mostly very large pine trees and the trail was mostly up hill, to Clingmans Dome, at 6,643 feet the highest point on the A.T. Snow was anywhere from an inch to three inches, and slush, and mud. There was a much better likelihood of seeing a snow snake than a rattlesnake. After another mile, the windfalls were every two to three hundred feet. Enormous trees, 30 to 40 inches on the butt, millions of board feet of lumber that would lay there and rot. Some I detoured around, some I went over and some I would take my pack off and throw it over the downed tree and crawl under the darn thing. At the last shelter, I read in the logbook an entry from Moose Head, it said among other things, "Life is good on the A.T." He had not yet been on this part of the trail. I laughed as I, 57 years old, crawled on my hands and knees in the slush and mud under another pine tree, rain gear ripping, my hat coming off, sweat running in my eyes, yes, life on the A.T. was definitely good. It took me 11 hours to hike the ten miles out to Newfound Gap, Sandy was there waiting. Two nights in Cherokee, it could not have come too soon.

A day in town was just what I needed. Having spent 21 days on the trail and covering 203 miles giving me only 19 days to complete my planned 500 mile trek.

I needed to average 15 miles per day to meet my goal. After a lousy breakfast at Big Boy in Cherokee, Sandy, my very understanding wife who I would not see again for 22 days dropped me off at the trailhead. The temperature read 45 degrees with a clear sky and I was eager to get going. With 30 miles left in the Smokies, the plan was to cover it in two days.

The day remained cool and dry, only the snow on the ground, at times six inches of it and a few windfalls reminded me of the storm that besieged the Smokies just days earlier. I met two youthful southbound day hikers and they called me "sir," my white scraggly whiskers must not be doing anything to make me look younger. Sandy was kind of expecting a Kenny Rogers look but what she got was more the Ted Kaczynski experience. I made good time, over 15 miles in seven hours and felt like doing more. It was my best day on the trail. I hope that it was a sign of things to come.

Another overfilled shelter last night with lots of snoring and again very little sleep. To get out of the Smokies I will do 20 miles today, a milestone, if it does not kill me. I want to start sleeping in my tent again. Last night the guy sleeping next to me ditched his toothbrush four days ago thinking it weighed too much.

Around noon, I met a dozen horses on the trail. This is the only section of the A.T. they can legally use. What a mess, with the rain and snow of late they were sinking six inches into the mud. Not much fun hiking in that muddle. It is a great national park but it will be so good to get out of the Smokies. Moreover, I did not know how good it would be. Two miles out of the park as the trail goes under Interstate 40, a perfect place for trail magic. Down to 1,500 feet, the temperature soared to at least 70 degrees. A couple from the Ashville, N.C. area had a food table set up becoming a king. We dined on sloppy joes, fried potatoes, and many different types of fruit and drinks. There is an exceptional place in heaven for people that take a day out of their lives and spend it feeding hikers. I hope they know how much it is appreciated.

Back on the trail with a very full belly and still three uphill miles to go before camping. Having been out here now for over 20 days the scenery for the most part does not get me very excited. I look off to the side now and again but for the most part my focus is on the next step. My heavy leather boots seem to be doing a good job protecting my weak ankles. Our thirty-ninth wedding anniversary is fast approaching, April 27. I must remember to get and mail a card in Hot Springs. I picked up a six-inch piece of tree bark and put it in my pocket to serve as a reminder.

Tree Whisperer was at the same camping area. He sleeps in a hammock and talks to the owls. Other than that, he seems normal. I believe he had three of them chatting last night, after a while they sound more like monkeys than owls. Fun to listen to.

Up early the next day after sleeping soundly for eleven hours. Today will be 18 miles and then 13 the next putting me in Hot Springs, N.C. around noon. It is amazing that I now look at 13 miles as a short day. The night before Tree Whisperer asked if I had any

Preparation-H and I did. He seemed very pleased to get it. When he returned it he said, "I thought one of you old guys might have some." I guess I should check my first-aid kit; I might have too much stuff in there.

Having been only a few days since my last shower but with warmer temperatures my body certainly puts out a rank odor, especially in my tent at night. Makes me wonder how the old cowboys or the lumberjacks ever did it.

Tree Whisperer and I walked into Hot Springs in the early afternoon, stopping at the first restaurant we came to and ordered the pot roast special. It was agreed there was nothing special about it but it was real food so no complaints were lodged. Finding a place to stay was not a problem, we walked across the street to the Sunnybank Inn, a white Victorian house, turned hostel, owned and operated by Elmer Hall. What a place, it could be best described as a lived in antique shop, and what a deal. For 15 bucks, you get a bed in a semi private room, and you get to take a shower. A vegetarian dinner for ten dollars is optional although you would have to be wacky not to take part. The atmosphere is definitely far left wing. I read in one of the trail guides that the Inn provided a progressive library. Most of the hostels and bunkhouses along the trail provide Backpacker and Readers Digest magazines for your reading pleasure. Sunnybank had perhaps a thousand-volume library, and yes, very liberal. I found nothing on the many shelves by the likes of Newt Gingrich, Bill O'Reilly, or anyone the least bit conservative. I am glad I knew this as I removed the

"Bush-Cheney" bumper sticker off my pack before I went in to register.

I guess there were eight of us hikers that opted for the vegetarian dinner plus three or four regulars that seemed to be either long-term guests or perhaps permanent residents. Near the conclusion of one of the finest meals I have ever eaten one of the regulars asked of no one in particular if we would like to listen to some music. Hearing no objections, he put on a Pete Seeger record. Yes, vinyl, on a record player. This young man seemed to be a huge fan of Pete's. He also happened to be a spokesperson or at least an activist for the movement to remove chlorine from drinking water. I mentioned to him that my dentist recommends that I not drink bottled water because of the need for chlorine to keep my teeth strong. He went into an extended and well-prepared sermon about the evils of chlorine, using many words I have never heard before so I let it pass.

As we sat there eating a very tasty desert, I have no idea what it was, listening to Pete sing protest songs on the record player my thoughts went back to the sixties. I was probably the only one there to have lived through them. If you ever get to Hot Springs, N.C., stay at Sunnybank, it is worth the 15 bucks.

A good night's sleep in a warm bed is always good but in the morning it was back on the trail and I must have been the first out of town as I had the privilege of breaking all the cobwebs that got spun across the trail last night. I walked for over an hour, mostly straight up and I could still see the little town of Hot Springs behind me. I also saw my first rattlesnake, about 18 inches long. I flipped him off the trail with my trekking pole and moved on, doing 20 miles that day. My next town stop will be Erwin, Tennessee, some 68 miles to the north. I need to do this stretch in four days, as Tom from Michigan will meet me there. The days were tough but passed quickly. After coming this far, I believe I could physically hike all the way to Maine but have reservations about handling the mental aspect of it. It is also becoming apparent there is not a mountain in the entire Appalachian Chain that will go unclimbed. I have not noticed much in the way of wildlife, mostly songbirds and squirrels but a few rabbits and a couple turkeys. One late afternoon it started raining almost immediately after setting my tent up so I committed the Cardinal sin of backpacking and cooked in my tent. Nothing happened, the tent did not burn down and no bears came that night, and I stayed dry. On my last day into Erwin most of my food is gone so the pack is light and I make 13 miles in less than six hours. I stepped out of the woods at Uncle Johnny's, an outfitter and hostel operator. There was an option to stay at Johnny's but I wanted to go into town, a few miles away. After walking about a mile an older couple that had been out, as they put it, "yard sailing" picked me up. I opened the door only to find the back seat full of stuff, yard sale stuff. "Just push it aside," the old guy instructed. They dropped me off in the downtown area where my objective was to find the famous Miss Janet's Bunkhouse. I stopped the first person I encountered to ask directions, something you would not catch me doing when driving a car. It would have been easy to walk right past the place, there were three cars parked in the yard, on the grass, not in the driveway, the yard, and the enormous front porch was just full of things, as if maybe they were having a yard sale. The place was almost full so I ended up with a top bunk, one of six beds in a 10X10 foot room that also contained a big over stuffed lazy-boy. Not a bad deal though, 20 bucks for the bunk, a shower, use of the washer and dryer and kitchen privileges and in the TV room there must have been 500 video cassettes. Some dating back to the 1970s, and friendly people, what a place. One of my favorites on the trail.

Within an hour my clothes and myself were washed and dried so I walked back to a Mexican restaurant the old guy pointed out on my ride into town. This would prove to be a colossal mistake, not that the food was bad but the gas it would produce in a 10X10 foot room that night. Feeling good, I then walked over to McDonalds for a chocolate shake. The rest of the afternoon was spent making phone calls, writing in my journal and watching old movies with five other hikers. About 8 PM, they put "Lonesome Dove," the six hour made for TV movie in the VCR. I read the book and saw the movie about 20 years ago. After about an hour it was bedtime for this tired hiker. The gas was already starting to work

49

but I was cleverly letting it slide out quietly and un-noticed. By ten, sleep had still not come my way and there was nothing quiet or un-noticed about the whole gas thing. I held most of it in until about 10:30 when I had to get up. Fortunately, the bathroom was right across the hall and better yet, it had a fart fan. No kidding, I released gas continuously for 30 seconds. What that burrito was made of remains a mystery. Thinking I owed it to my bunkmates to stay away for a while, I went and watched the end of Lonesome Dove.

Tom, my friend from Michigan picked me up at McDonalds in the early afternoon of the next day. We went back over to Uncle Johnny's where he provided long-term parking and a shuttle service that Tom planned to use after about two weeks of hiking. I had not hiked with Tom before and did not know what to expect. After a quick look at the maps, we decided our next re-supply would be Damascus, Virginia, some 120 miles north. My first thought was, "How in the hell will I carry that much food." I had enough provisions in my pack to last about six days so I bought two more days worth at Uncle Johnny's. Once we got off the road and onto the trail, Tom was gone, like the Energizer Bunny, just gone. I thought maybe I should go back to Uncle Johnny's and return the extra food I just bought because at the speed my new hiking partner was going we would be in Damascus in about four days. We only planned on going 5 miles that afternoon and when I arrived at Curley Maple Gap Shelter Tom was sitting there with a little grin on his face. "I usually don't hike that fast," he told me. "I just had a little nervous energy to burn off." I took a sigh of relief and started to pitch my tent.

Sitting around the campfire that night the discussion again turned to gear, it was a favorite subject for most of us. Low Branch told us his pack now weighed about 25 pounds and once the threat of cold weather passed he would bring it down to 18 pounds. I to d him my wife's purse weighs more than that. Most of us there were "On the Road to Damascus," and of course, that meant heavy food bags. Some of us would make it in six or seven days but for slower hikers it could take 10. It was the consensus of all of us that a Shoney's Restaurant at every road crossing would be a good thing. An older hiker, in his mid 60's added that there was no such thing as getting in shape, his whole body hurt every day. Another guy informed me that my tent looked more like a small mobile home. It was large compared to most others, weighing almost four and a half pounds and will be replaced before coming back next year. Of course, we talked about what motivated us to do this, walking on a trail in the forest, some covering over 2,000 miles in five months. Some were between jobs, some retired, looking for one last adventure while they were still able, many students looking for one last quest before settling down, a few were running away while others were just looking for answers to questions they were not quite sure of. Tom is a hiker; he has hiked all over the country. He has been to the summit of Katahdin and the floor of the Grand Canyon; his friends tell him he takes weird vacations.

My reasoning is that because at 57 years of age, I do not have the option of putting it off much longer. Not needing a reason to do this other than simply wanting to do it but mostly I am here because rational thinking has never been my strong suit. No one does this for money and not for fame as thousands have preceded us but merely for the experience and to savor the memories. When you reach that certain age, it is different for everyone, you realize you no longer have the ambition to undertake a big expedition, the big excursions are out of reach but then again maybe they always were so you find something you like and do it. Sometimes I think I'm afraid of getting old but am probably mistaken, it is not getting old that frightens me, although the idea of sitting in a Lazy-Boy waiting for it does. I am not much for fishing and I cannot play golf, although I have tried. I could not think of any good reasons not to go and it sounded like a great adventure. So far, I have been right.

The next morning Tom hit the trail 20 minutes before I started out. This would set a precedent for the rest of our time on the trail. I tried to have oatmeal and coffee in the morning where Tom would pack up and leave, eating a granola bar as he walked. After five miles or so I would catch him and there a plan would be made for the rest of the day, agreeing to camp at a particular place that evening. There might be one or even three more meeting but for the most part, we hiked alone. The first full day covered over 16 miles and in the first ten it was an elevation rise of over 2,000 feet, and straight up the side of Unaka Mountain. At least it felt that way, most places used switchbacks to do any serious climbing but the switchback engineer must have been off sick the day they laid this one out and his assistant told the crew to, "Ah hell, just run her straight up to the top."

The day after Unaka Mountain came Roan Mountain, sometimes referred to as "Groan Mountain," another 2,000-foot elevation rise. It was hot, in the 80's; after reaching the summit, I went over and sat in the shade on a picnic table. Yes, most people drive their cars up there; a few of us walk. Two Forest Service workers were up there getting the toilets ready for the summer season. One of them must have felt sorry for this old white bearded guy because he gave me two bottles of ice-cold water. Thank you very much. I sat and drank that cold bottle of water in celebration, not that I had climbed Roan Mountain but that I did not have to do it again. That 15-mile day was arguably my hardest day to this point. This trail does not let you forget your age, Roan Mountain reaffirmed that I was much closer to a casket than the cradle.

The first day of May, the handle on my water filter broke, plastic, made in Switzerland. It was still usable but not very convenient. I hope that an outfitter in Damascus will be able to replace it. We did about 15 miles and stopped for a swim in the Elk River, very cold water but it sure felt good. We camped a short distance from there. It now seems like my thoughts are concentrated on food, real food, not the kind we are eating on the trail. I told Tom that when we get to

Damascus I was going to walk down one side of the street and visit every restaurant. Then I would turn around, come down the other side, and stop at every other one. My weight must be down about ten pounds so far, my belt buckle even turns in at the top. Jenny Craig would go out of business if everyone did this.

We camped in a grassy field above the river. At 2:30 the next morning, I crawled out of my tent to go pee, an event that takes place just like clockwork. Down by the river I noticed a headlight moving around, thinking it was someone getting prepared to do some night hiking I got the great idea that maybe we should also do a night hike. I woke Tom up and ran the suggestion past him, he's crazy, we were packed up and moving in 30 minutes. Come to find out the light by the river was from a young guy just setting his tent up, he had done 30 miles and thought he would stop and rest a bit.

With the increased mileage, blisters on my feet are starting to become a problem. Band-aids cover every other toe with duck tape on my heels. At Dennis Cove Road, we had the option of walking a quarter mile on the blacktop to Kincora Hiking Hostel, a bunkhouse that also provided a shuttle into a small town. Pizza and cold Diet Coke never tasted so good. The bunkhouse was filled near capacity but we scored bunks in the upstairs level of the building. It was very hot and a small window fan provided little relief, I thought about pitching my tent in the back yard but let it pass. This would be my last bunkhouse if I could help it. Again, finding sleep hard to come by we started

54

hiking at 3 AM. It was a tough 18 miles to the Vandeventer Shelter and the threat of rain convinced us to spend the night with a tin roof over our heads. I believe this is only the third occasion I have taken advantage of the shelters. A good place as far as getting out of the weather but you also become a captive audience as would be the case with a young guy from New York who was upset because some Mom and Pop grocery store in Tennessee did not carry his preferred brand of veggie dip. He was so disturbed about it that he talked to the store manager. Two other guys were going on about cell phone use. In my 43 days on the trail, I saw no one abuse the use of cell phones. By that, I mean no one used them in a shelter, at a picnic table, or around a campfire. It was not unusual to come across hikers sitting on a log by the trail, usually at a higher elevation having a conversation with someone back in the real world. Most of the hikers voicing displeasure with cell phones were young, probably with little or no responsibility back home. Perhaps some of them, in their heads were on some sort of Lewis and Clark expedition and wanted this to be as macho as possible. If you are going on the trail, take your cell phone, if you do not have one, get one. It is a safety thing.

The day before getting to Damascus, we did 22 miles over moderately rolling terrain. Not a bad day for two old guys. Our last day into town would be a short mostly downhill ten miles. The thought of restaurant food and another zero day always provides incentive to start moving it the morning. Damascus bills itself as the friendliest town on the A.T. and from what I have seen thus far it cannot be argued with. However, it is not the cheapest; there are no inexpensive motels and no fast food joints. For the budget minded, there are bunkhouses but after that, you are left to one of the many Bed and Breakfasts that line Laurel Avenue. The name of the B&B we stayed at was not recorded in my journal but it was a great place and included breakfast. Maybe five other north bounders were there including 501 who we would see for the last time. Bob, his real name is a hiker's hiker that seemed to enjoy every step he took. I stopped at the Mt. Rogers Outfitters with my water filter and they replaced the broken part at no cost. Talk about customer service, the thing was purchased in Atlanta. Tom is not feeling well, some sort of flu bug. Here we are in town and the poor guy cannot eat, everyone that finds out about this feels bad for him. Two of the meals I ate in town were Italian; after all the bitching about eating pasta on the trail, I cannot explain it. On May 7, I solo hiked out of Damascus; Tom was still not feeling up to the trail. He would take one more zero day, then catch a shuttle, and meet me about 20 miles up the trail.

The first day from town, 16 miles in seven hours with well-rested legs came easy. That night I surgically removed, with my Leatherman, the nail on my little toe. There was no blood so it must have been ready to come off.

The next day required a climb up White Top Mountain, the second highest point in Virginia. Just speculating but it most likely acquired its name from the petite white flowers that grow there. It actually looked like snow on the ground; they were that dense. Marching down the back side, I met two south bounders, a man and woman. Thinking it would be the right thing to do, I stepped off the trail to allow them passage. The woman, 20 feet ahead of the guy stopped right next to me. "You are trampling the wildflowers," she informed me. I was taken aback as there were wildflowers everywhere but on the trail itself. To not stand on the darn flowers would have required me to either levitate or shimmy up a tree. Before she could walk on, I mumbled something like, "Well, there are a lot of them." Her companion, the dutiful husband said nothing as he passed. And they let people like that vote.

Tom was waiting for me a couple miles up the trail and we ambled on, our days on the trail were getting short. The vistas in Virginia were equivalent to or better than any I have yet seen on the trail. It reminded me of the old west TV shows I watched back in the 50's and 60's. The day turned out beautiful although last night was another cold one, at 3:30 AM I put my rain gear on to stay warm. As the hike progresses, my thoughts turn from food to pack weight. I have concluded that the only difference between a 42-pound pack and a 32-pound pack is a little knowledge and a lot of money. Sandy will be happy to hear that.

Rather than getting off the trail after 40 days and riding the Greyhound home Sandy will pick us up in Atkins, Virginia on May 13. We have slowed our

57

mileage as to not over hike our pick-up point. Doing ten miles a day when your body will do 18 is somewhat of a shock. After stopping at the 500-mile mark and posing for pictures, it was a quick walk to Dickey Gap. From there we hitched a ride into Troutdale and enjoyed a very good meal at Jerry's Kitchen. The cool morning turned into a very hot, sticky day. Back on the trail a young hiker passed me and did he ever smell, I am being polite, he just good old fashion stunk. Four days out of Damascus and my own body smelled kind of ripe but this guy must have walked right through town without bothering himself with a little water and a bar of soap. There was a halo of fly's buzzing around his head.

We came across another "personality," Tyvek Man. Tyvek is a house wrap used by building contractors, as far as I know, when wrapped completely around a house it allows it to "breath." It is incredibly tough and very lightweight so it also makes a good ground cloth for backpacker's tents. Tyvek Man went the extra step and made all his clothes out of the material and he was barefooted.

Around noon on my 41st day on the trail we walked into the Partnership shelter, perhaps the best I have seen this far. The shelter was located only a few hundred yards from Mt. Rogers National Recreation Area Headquarters. Not a big deal except Pizza Hut delivered and whoever is responsible for the shower may you have a long and happy life and when your days on this earth are over I am sure there will be a special place in Heaven for you. A big thank you from all us hikers that last had a shower in Damascus.

We spent one more night on the trail, at the Chartfield Shelter. Tent sites were at a minimum and the one I selected was by far the most un-level of the entire excursion. Every bit of clothes I have on is made of nylon or some other slippery material. My tent floor is made of something slippery as is my sleeping bag, put this all together and I had one hell of a night just trying to stay in my tent. The next morning we hiked less than five miles to Atkins and rented a cheap room at the Relax Inn, 45 bucks for the night. A little mold growing in the bathroom but the bed was level and had no rocks under the mattress. After showers, we walked over to "The Barn" restaurant for as much real food as our stomachs could hold. When paying the bill I thumbed through a hiker logbook laying on the counter, I found this entry from Tyvek Man, "If you are not living on the edge, you are taking up to much room."

Sandy picked us up the next day; we dropped Tom off at his truck in Erwin. Farewells were said with plans to come back next year and, "do another 500."

August first, 2007. It has been about 75 day's since leaving the trail and like marathon runners; I undeniably had a slight case of post event depression. It has been good to get back into a routine that did not include sleeping in a tent and walking 15 miles a day. People are no longer asking, "How many miles today." My body has reclaimed nine of the 20 pounds that melted away on the trail. Oatmeal has no place on my

59

breakfast table, having eaten it 43 days straight was enough and I fancy ice in my drinking water. The little toe on my left foot has not healed completely but looks better every day. This fall when they go on sale the purchase of a new and lighter tent, backpack, and sleeping bag will be in order. Right after returning home, I was the high bidder for a postal type scale on E-Bay. No more 42-pound packs, the exact weight of every item I carry will now be logged. Almost daily, I go to WhiteBlaze.com to check the progress of friends that remain on the trail. White Bear and Cojo, a couple from Atlanta and Kimmi and Trevor from Seattle have dropped off. Leonard, my friend from Rocky Mountain, Walker, Jea, Low Branch and 501 continue on. Glen, "Tree Whisperer" has not made an entry in over a month but I am hoping he is still marching north.

Chapter Two

April 22, 2008

Atkins, Virginia to Just North of Harpers Ferry

The Virginia Blues

       Sandy dropped me off at the Relax Inn just off of I-81 near Atkins, Virginia. Tom made reservations two weeks ago however it looked to be un-necessary as there were no additional vehicles in the parking lot. I picked up the room key from the same woman that worked the reception desk the previous year. This was our stopping point after last year's 43-day 535-mile hike from Springer Mountain in Georgia. Sandy walked into room number 6 behind me, the same room Tom and I occupied last year and before dropping my backpack she allowed it to be known that she would not spend the night in a "place like this." It was good for a chuckle and after a brief inspection I noticed the "see through" towels from last year had been replaced but the black stuff was still growing like a hard to kill weed in certain areas of the bathroom. Don't take this as complaining as hiker motels are just that, a somewhat economical place for long distance hikers to get a shower, wash clothes, recharge the cell phone battery, and spend a night out of the elements. At 45 dollars split between two guys it is not a bad deal and I have stayed in a couple far worse.

Sandy left to return home and with Tom still three hours away there was little to occupy my time other than the Weather Channel on a 14-inch screen and my thoughts. I have looked forward to this day with great anticipation since we ended our hike almost a year ago. My last year's backpack with five days food and 40 ounces of water weighed in at 45 pounds. This year a new "Go Lite" back pack, a down sleeping bag guaranteed to keep you alive but not necessarily comfortable down to 40 degrees and a much lighter albeit smaller tent my pack this year will weigh no more than 32 pounds. It is amazing what a few well-spent dollars and more importantly the blessings of my wife did to lighten the load. We heard last year from south bounders, people hiking the trail north to south that the trail would get easier as we progressed into Virginia but that turned out to be fictional. Other than the one hundred or so miles in the Shenandoah National Park the Appalachian is a very demanding trail in Virginia.

Long distance hikers are few in numbers and

each of us is motivated by a healthy appetite for the extreme. We are normal, for the most part. We play golf; fish, go bowling, and watch the news on TV but there forever seems to be an itch that needs to be scratched. The discovery a new tent that weighs two ounces less than the one used last year gets us excited. A good deal of thought goes into dumping the old Katadyn water filter in favor of the much lighter Aqua Mura treatment system. The lure of this trail or that trail is always hibernating in the back of one's mind.

I suppose this would be a good time to offer you even a modest amount of information regarding the small rural communities and villages we hikers pass through. For the most part, they are nondescript, a few on their deathbed but most seem to be keeping one foot ahead of the undertaker and all are blessed with an abundance of very friendly and helpful people. Some have more empty storefronts than not, a hiker motel, a grocery store and hopefully a post office and Laundromat being the most important to us hikers. Perhaps the folks living here in the south would drive an American made car or even more so a Ford or Chevrolet pick-up truck. I would venture they know how to repair them and furthermore not afraid to pick up five stinking hikers and ferry them into town. They are the kind of people that could fix an electrical or plumbing problem in their homes and have a neighbor that would lend a hand. It is just my opinion but these are the people that make America the great country it is.

Tom arrived about 4 P.M. with cloudy skies

overhead but with his customary sunny disposition. It was a quick walk three hundred yards up hill to the "Barn," a large red painted wood-sided building masquerading as a restaurant. It is a colossal hit with hikers as the A.T. meanders within spitting distance of its front door. The food could not be served at a restaurant in Garrison Keillors Lake Wobegon as the chow is not above average and is worthy of few if any accolades but knowing that other than breakfast in the morning this will be our final chance at regular food for about five days. We ate like lumberjacks and left a too large tip for the middling service rendered.

Our opening day on the trail began with a no alarm needed 6 A.M. wake up and a speedy trip back to the Barn for breakfast. On the trail at 7:15 and at 7:17 we stopped for the first of countless photo ops with our new-fangled digital cameras. It seemed that either one of us was proficient with their workings but with only a few buttons to push, Tom quickly figured them out. The heavens were overcast causing the air to be clammy with the threat of rain but it mattered little, after nearly a 12-month absence Tom and Buck were back on the Appalachian Trail and would remain so for the next six weeks. We were prepared for anything Mother Nature could throw at us. The first mile and a half started out exceptionally flat. With the adrenalin pumping it passed very quickly but soon the trail started going up and in my psyche I soon remembered what this path is all about but it was evident my legs would need to be re-introduced to the task at hand. Our first rest stop came at the Davis Path Shelter and there we had the privilege of meeting our first through hiker. A young man in his early twenties introduced himself as "Tupperware" so I had to ask, "How did ya come by that name."

"It goes back to my college days," he replied. "I shared a two bedroom one bathroom apartment with a buddy and one evening after a night out at a local Mexican restaurant I got the urge to relieve some of the anxiety building up in my gut. My roommate was already in the bathroom dealing with his own business and I just could not wait a minute longer so I did the obvious, I found the biggest Tupperware container we had and did my job right there in the kitchen. Tupperware has been my name ever since."

This would be the last time we would see him, as he was young and doing big miles but his story was good for a laugh. After wishing him well he set off on his pursuit of Mt. Katahdin. Tupperware would only be the first of several interesting and amusing hikers and town folks encountered in the next 40 days.

At mile six came the first of numerous thousand-foot peaks, fortunately the trail builders were incredibly generous with the switchbacks and even with our rookie legs, it seemed to be an easy climb. Our next stop came at the Knot Maul Shelter, according to the Appalachian Trail Thru-Hikers' Companion it was named for the knotty wood early settlers used as mauls for their farm work. There we met a man in his early 60's, a potential thru-hiker from South Carolina. He went by the trail name of Tenderfoot and even though I have lived in the south over 20 years at times I found myself missing some of the words that rolled off his tongue. Having been on the trail already for more than two months he looked somewhat skeletal sitting in the shelter smoking one of his off brand cigarettes. He told Tom and me that some of his friends back home placed limits on the probability of his reaching Katahdin and I said nothing of the sort but I too was in their camp. Forty days later standing at the train station in Harpers Ferry to catch my ride into Washington D.C., there stood Tenderfoot waiting to greet his daughter who would spend a few days with him as he rested up for his push into the second half of the trail. Tenderfoot was one of the hikers we would encounter frequently throughout our 40 day hike. After getting to know him I had few doubts of his successful journey to that mountain in Maine. A fine Southern gentleman who told us he was going to take a computer class when he got home, but he said it with a little chuckle as he lit up another smoke. He took my snail-mail address and promised to drop me a line upon completion of the trail.

After a very respectable 14 miles that first day we pitched our tents at Lynn Camp Creek. The night stayed warm, too much so for my 40 degree sleeping bag but without it I was cold. Tom had the same problem so at 5 A.M. it was out of our tents and at 5:30 walking with headlights burning. We did something that day to unknowingly prove that adrenalin runs longer than the first day. The two old guys from Michigan walked 19 miles and that included a 2,000 foot ascent to Chestnut Knob Shelter. It seemed our mindset was that as long as there was daylight our legs would keep working. I cannot imagine why two 58 year old men would assume such a thing. That evening while sitting on a log at the Jenkins Shelter eating instant mashed potatoes and gravy Tom advised me one of his goals during the journey would be to come up with a reasonable explanation of what motivated him to hike this trail. Replying that I would squander no time on such thoughts, as it would probably scare the hell out of me if I knew what the inspiration was behind this hike. For me some things are best left unknown but I wished him well in his thoughts.

It was early in the trip this year but I could see a pattern developing. It would be that of Felix Unger and Oscar Madison, the Odd Couple and anyone that has known me even briefly will tell you I would be the unorganized unkempt Oscar Madison while Tom would easily fill the role of Felix. Tom keeps detailed notes of such things as trail conditions, calories consumed in a 24 hour period and specific events that highlight each day on the trail. He combs his hair every morning and always seems to have a clean t-shirt to put on before walking into town. His backpack is well organized and always neatly packed. He knows how much food we will need between re-supplies and tells me almost to the minute what time we will get to the grocery store 80 miles up the trail. I am grateful for all this as last year while hiking alone I always had eight days of provisions in my pack. Every town close to the trail simply meant buying eight more days worth of food. It did not appear to worry him that at night when we hoist our bear bags in a tree that I hold back a few candy bars to munch on during the night. Pitching my tent so that it does not appear to be an old swayback horse gives me the fits while his looks like the ones you see on the cover of Cabela's catalog. At the conclusion of a hard day after camp is made and supper eaten, if enough daylight remains Tom likes to go for a walk. I on the other hand lay in my tent eating candy bars. Get the picture? I could probably do this hike alone but with much more difficulty and it would not be nearly as much fun.

The next morning greeted me with a tender right knee, no doubt an overuse injury the result of our 19 mile hike the day before. My meager first-aid kit contained approximately 30 Aleve pain killers and I would devour every one of them during the next week before this painful injury magically disappeared.

Our third day on the trail was the first I was able to call home on my cell phone. Verizon's coverage on the trail would prove to be second rate at best. At 12:30 that afternoon we came to U.S. 21/52 where we proudly raised our thumbs and in that all American tradition hitched a three mile ride into the small Village of Bland. We started with light food packs knowing we could re-supply after only 45 miles of hiking. In reality we walked the first mile on very hot asphalt but then got a ride from a guy in a pickup truck. On the outskirts of town we came to an abrupt halt, as there on the road stood a fifteen hundred pound cow blocking traffic in both directions. Our driver got out as did we and together with the cow's owner and two other towns' people the big girl was persuaded back into her pasture. We walked from there to a neighborhood restaurant located in the back of a gas station and dined on all you can eat hamburger steak, beans, potato salad and dinner rolls. The hamburger stake was only slightly more tender than my Argentinean made beef jerky but for $5.49 no one complained. From there a short walk around the corner put us at the IGA where our food bags were re-supplied and then it was ice cream cones on the park bench in front of the store. Good fortune was in our corner as it was there we met "Kimo" and "Free Hugs." They had a car and of course offered us a ride back to the trail. Kimo, an older balding man started hiking the trail with a 50 mile section back in 1967. He then took 30 years of zeros, no hiking at all but eventual resumed his quest to complete the trail in 1997. With only 600 miles remaining he thought three years would be enough to finish the job. His plan this year was to park his car in town, shuttle 200 miles north, and hike south bound until he returned to Bland. We met him once more about 120 miles north of Bland in the Tinker Cliffs area. "Free Hugs," a young man with longer hair and a full beard is an Iraq War Veteran who carries steel shrapnel in his head that caused him to be medically discharged from the Army. A potential through hiker he is a recent graduate from a wood working school that deals with high end furniture. He hopes to open his own shop this fall upon completion of this hike. We were able to stay with Free Hugs for a few days but before long his young legs out ran our old ones but we kept track of his progress in the shelter logs. Kimo and Free Hugs are a good example of the age differentials to be found on the trail. Kimo was probably born during the Roosevelt Administration and Free Hugs came into the world when Ronald Reagan occupied the White House but both pursued the same dream of becoming a thru hiker. After a more reasonably 13 miles we spent the night at Helvey's Mill Shelter. A quick word about some shelters; the walls of some of these buildings remind me of the walls in restrooms of gas stations in the seedy part of town. You can only wonder what these people are thinking but then again I doubt they are thinking at all. You dim-witted guys that feel it is necessary to write or carve your name or your girlfriends name on the shelter walls need to get a life.

Another humid night, the 40 degree sleeping bag is looking to be a smart move but we know not what the future holds. Our fourth day the maps tell us there is no water on the first ten miles of the trail. Hiking out of camp that morning with full water bottles plus the weight of the provisions purchased yesterday in Bland makes for a heavy load. At 9 A.M. big time clouds rolled in with all the makings of a morning thunderstorm. We quickly donned our rain gear and added covers to our packs. After walking all of a quarter mile the clouds vanished making way for the sun to again fill the sky. It made for a good laugh as we removed our rain gear, another lesson from Mother Nature regarding life on the trail. We stopped at Jenny Knob Shelter for lunch. I should add that again this year Tom and I seldom hike together, I am a little faster on the up hills but in the rocky sections, and there are many of them Tom seems to sashay over and through them while I stumble and trip on every other one of them. Before setting out in the morning a rendezvous point is selected where a snack might be eaten and more plans discussed. Again this year it seems the two of us are never more than ten minutes away from each other. Somewhere on the trail that day I met Melt Down, a young college student from Vermont whose next re-supply will be Pearisburg, Virginia, some 40 miles to the north and that will put him at 12 days without a shower. That evening we camped at the Kimberling Creek suspension bridge. The bridge spans some 150 feet over the lazy, bucolic Kimberling Creek and the area offers some reasonably level tent sites but they are close to the road, Virginia 606. After four days walking in humid weather conditions the thought of washing up in the river was rather appealing. I removed my boots and socks and slid into my Crocks, actually a cheap 12 dollar knock off from Wal-Mart and walked into the cool slow moving trout stream. About knee deep I stepped onto a flat but slippery rock and promptly fell on my butt. Nothing injured other than my pride. I recovered quickly and looked around for witnesses, there were none but I did tell Tom what happened. The sun was still turning out enough BTU's that enabled me to dry my clothing by hanging them on small underbrush near my tent. We did 16 miles today but discussed slowing down a little as my knee becomes very painful later in the day. It is particularly bothersome on the down hills; I have it wrapped with an Ace bandage but am starting to consider the probability of this thing chasing me off the trail.

We slept late on day five not getting on the trail until approximately 7 A.M. After hiking only a short distance; maybe a half mile when we found Tender Foot and Free Hugs camped on a steep hillside. I am positive they rested little last night as a level tent site is of the utmost importance. A little afterward we passed the 600 mile mark, the total mileage from Springer Mountain in Georgia. It was a mini milestone for us or perhaps a mini miracle as the adrenalin was with us no longer and our legs were starting to act their age. I told Tom that even a dog will lay down when he's tired but we keep pushing, knowing that tomorrow we will be in Pearisburg, Virginia and the thought of our first zero day is great motivation. I had three bars on the cell phone and called Sandy, she informed me an old friend died back in Michigan. Ed Heikkila was in his early 80's, a great sportsman but an even better teller of tales. The woodlands in the Central Upper Peninsula will forever be less than whole with Ed's passing. I see Ed's character traits in some of the through hikers I have met on the trail and they are the ones I lay my money on making it to Katahdin.

We took a long break at Wapiti Shelter as a 1,200 foot climb is next on the agenda. I automatically hope for a well laid out trail with switchbacks but the total distance is barely two miles so it could be as the crow flies up the side of the mountain. Nevertheless, it really makes no difference, the trail is the trail, and it is not an easy thing to accomplish.

Elk, (wapiti) wandered this locale in the not to distance past, as did timber wolves, bison, and mountain lions but I have no idea why they are no longer here. After 12 miles we pitched our tents right in the middle of a forest service road used only for fighting fires. This happened after walking half a mile down that road to fill our water bottles. At the spring was an abandoned building, perhaps an old homestead, rain was threatening and I mentioned to Tom that it looked like the doors were not locked and maybe it would make a good place to spend the night. All he said was, "Looks like a good place for rats and rattlesnakes to me." I'm so lucky to be hiking with him; we set our tents up as described before. It did rain but I shared my tent with neither rat nor rattlesnake.

With clearing skies in the morning our hike began at 6 A.M. Doc's Knob Shelter was our stopping point for lunch. The Lady and the Tramp, both registered nurses from Arizona and prospective thru hikers were also there. It seemed they were a little reluctant to divulge their medical field experience as the last thing they wanted to do was look at blistered feet every day. We hiked with them for the next week.

Shortly after noon the asphalt road to Pearisburg became our new trail. It was a short one mile walk into town, it could not come soon enough as my knee was getting downright ugly and I hoped the day and a half off would provide some relief. The Plaza Motel would be our home, 42 bucks for two beds and it included laundry. The room was clean, the TV worked and a Chinese and Italian restaurant were close by. The next day turned cold and the rain came in buckets, an excellent time for a zero day. It was spent grocery shopping, picking up a mail drop from the post office, and purchasing a patella knee strap from the pharmacy. There were several other hikers using them and I believe it helped. We also made a resolution to slow down and hike fewer miles. Of course it was soon forgotten. Pearisburg, as is most of Virginia, historical. It is noted on a large sign that in May of 1862, Confederates under General Henry Heth defeated Union troops under Colonel Rutherford B. Hays. The city was celebrating its bicentennial this summer, 2008.

Having lived in Michigan's Upper Peninsula for many years, I remember in the spring of each year everyone would wait to see our first Robin, a sure indication that winter was over. It made me wonder if the folks living along the A.T. waited for the first through hikers to start marching the streets of their villages, knowing warm weather would soon follow.

Warm weather was not on the menu our first day out of Pearisburg. After breakfast at Hardees, 35-degree temperature and 20 mile an hour wind met us at the door. Today's march lasted only about 12 miles before stopping to set up camp. Tonight will be a "three dog night" so preparations were taken and we hoped for a little reprieve from Mother Nature. It did not happen; at 3 A.M., too cold to sleep our only choice was to start walking. It was a quick six miles to the Pine Swamp Branch Shelter before stopping to have breakfast. Soon after we met Ten-88, a thru hiking retired math professor, (Columbia University) from

74

New Jersey. He is a great guy with a quick wit. Our paths would cross several times in the next few weeks. I will add that he was hiking the trail in Crocks. There I am with blistered feet in my 170 dollar boots and he is doing the whole trail in 15-dollar Crocks. After getting home, I read his blog online and found that he recently lost an adult son to leukemia.

Today's tally read 18 miles and every hiker on the trail kept moving just to stay warm. The night was spent at the War Spur Shelter and it did warm up a little. Sleep came easy as it turned out to be a rough day, not only the walking but the cold weather seems to drain our strength.

Day ten, this marks the one-quarter mark of the trip. My knee has been one extreme to the next, at times almost normal but at others it seems the sand is about to run out of the hourglass. The night was spent at yet another shelter, so many are passed by that unless I have taken a picture they all seem similar but of course they are not as some are much more accommodating than others. Today was our first meeting with Cricket; the guy could have been Davy Crocket. An outdoorsman all his life he talks at length of hunting and trapping, making venison sausage, and a variety of other things. He was with the 101st Airborne in Viet Nam and then worked 37 years without missing a day's work for DuPont. Ten-88 hiked with him from their first days back in Georgia and on one occasion told his wife in a phone conversation that thanks to Cricket, "I now know how to skin a muskrat." About a week later, a fisherman gave him four fresh caught brook trout, which he promptly cooked over an open fire, Tom, and I shared in his good fortune. We hiked together about ten days but then he moved on at faster pace. I gave him my E-mail address and received a promise of a short note when he completes the trail. I am confident that sometime this fall Cricket will climb Mt. Katahdin.

Later that afternoon, only 20 feet off the trail I came upon a large Texas State flag fluttering in the wind. It was a monument to World War II hero Audie Murphy. He survived the Germans but died in a plane crash near this site in 1971

Day 11 turned warm and I was grateful but my knee was killing me and my feet were turning into yet another problem. I wore the same boots from last year but with a small altercation, arch supports. Three weeks before starting the hike, I came down with tendonitis in my right foot. The podiatrist gave me a shot of cortisone and sold me the supports for 50 bucks. All was fine until the hike started with a 32-pound pack on my back. The supports made my feet ride differently in the boots to the point of losing three toenails in the first 150 miles, plus numerous blisters. I also wondered if the supports were the source of my knee pain.

It was a tough 16 miles today but not because we wanted it to be. Late in the afternoon when our main concern should have been looking for a tent site, down the trail comes G.I. Joe, not his real name. Dressed fully in U.S. Army camouflage and diamond stud earrings the 35 to 40 year old survivalist seemed to be out on maneuvers, at least in his own mind or perhaps in his fantasy world. We asked where he planned to camp, wished him well and put four miles distance between us. Scared the hell out of us. The stealth campsite high on Cove Mountain more or less picked us rather than us picking it. The terrain was extremely rocky and not knowing what lie ahead, we settled in on what turned out to be our most un-level campsite of the entire trip. All night long, I kept sliding toward the back of my tent. It was warm but breezy and I slept little. At 3:30 A.M. it was back on the trail on what turned out to be an incredibly tough, rocky up and down seven-mile trudge into Catawba. A section of the trail notoriously known as the Dragons Tooth and another as Lost Spectacles Gap turned out to be some of the hardest hiking encountered this far and a large amount of it was done in darkness. We stepped onto Virginia 785 at 10:30 and quickly caught a ride to the post office. This was not a planned zero day but a nero day, thus the short mileage. Our first order of business was at the post office to pick up our mail drops. The guidebook listed only the Catawba General Store and the Homeplace Restaurant that featured all you can eat dining. A shower was high on the agenda but our prospects looked dim, no hostel, no motel, not much of anything in Catawba with the exception of a very kindhearted postmistress. Tom inquired if there was a place in town that catered to hikers, as we would like to clean up a bit before going to the restaurant. "No," she replied. "But wait a second, my husband is coming in now, he might take y'all up to the house for a shower."

"Certainly, come on, I'll run ya's up there right now." Was his comeback.

He was about five foot ten with a full beard and perhaps a little beer belly. I walked out with him and Tom stayed inside to mail a birthday card. I noticed on the back window of his pickup truck the U.S. Marine Corps logo stretching from one side to the other. He was about my age, 58 and I hoped he had a story so I mentioned the fact that he was a Marine, I was proud that I knew there are no former Marines. I think he also appreciated that and boy did he have a story, short but to the point he spoke directly, "I spent five years in Viet Nam, I'm a highly trained killer and I miss it immensely."

Just then Tom walked out of the Post Office and our highly trained killer motioned us toward the truck, "Jump in boys, I'll run ya's up to the house."

There was a dreadful smell about so we rode in the box. On the ride to the house I relayed to Tom what our drivers past involved and then I said, "I bet he's going to take us up to the house and kill us." Laughter broke out but it was an uneasy laugh, I just hoped he would let us take a shower first. While pulling into the driveway and before the truck stopped two mutt dogs that were very good at defending their territory welcomed us. Our driver yelled back at us to remain in the truck until he put the half-breads up. Once in the house, I took the shower off the hall and Tom got the master bath. The Marine furnished us with clean towels and made sure we had soap and shampoo. The shower was great even if I had to dress in my grimy clothes. I walked into the living room just as our friend fired up his pot pipe, which he was eager to share but we mutually declined. He then picked up a guitar and played us a song I have never heard before. After the one song concert it was back to town, this time riding in the cab. At first glance there is nothing in Catawba, Va. that would make you remember this little village but the kindheartedness shown by a postal employee and her long haired highly trained killer husband will make me remember this encounter for a long time to come. We left the post office in high spirits but did not know that Catawba was not yet done being kind to us. Just across the street sat an old time general store that stocked the things you would expect to find in such a place plus they had a small deli in the back but that is not all. In another building behind the store was a hostel of sorts with no amenities. Four walls, a roof and a floor made from plywood, an overhead florescent light, one door and one window in the back and it was free. That night I believe eight of us spent the night complements of the people that own the Catawba General Store. I washed some clothes with a garden hose and strung a rope between trees to dry them on. Later that afternoon around five several of us walked half a mile to the Homeplace Restaurant, home-style service with very good food. This little town turned out to be a real treasure along the trail. That evening Tom, Ten-88, Cricket and I sat in front of the hostel and watched as four young hikers played hacky sack. One of the young studs invited us old guys to join in. Ten-88 replied that our generation was more of the hula-hoop era and Cricket added that he knew what a Slinky was. The youngsters knew of the hula-hoop but the Slinky was a new word for them, it was worth a little chuckle from both camps. We slept soundly that night and walked out of town the next morning reassured that there were still some very good people left that will do things for strangers without expecting compensation.

The next morning on the road Tom and I walked the entire two and a half miles back to the trail. Sunday morning is not as good day for hitching a ride. Sometime today the 700-mile marker will greet us, 250 of those miles in Virginia, another milestone but the Virginia Blues are setting in. The trail has 550 miles in this state so another 300 remain, about 23 days worth of hiking. At McAfee Knob, hikers enjoy one of the finest panoramas of the whole excursion and it also marked our reunion with south bounder Kimo. Our next highlight is Tinkers Cliffs, a half-mile stretch of trail that I would not have felt safe on in the presence of a strong wind. The guidebook tells us that during the Revolutionary War deserters camped in this area and repaired pots and pans ("tinkers"). Walking the Cliffs I see mountains to my left and to the right, mountains behind and more ahead, when I close my eyes at night mountains materialize beneath my eyelids. If I ever get to Katahdin will there still be mountains to be climbed or will my thrust for such a life be satisfied? I have a hard time imagining people that do this trail more than once but most folks would not consider doing it even the first time. You could say it is foolish to be out here hiking and maybe it is but if you are inclined to do foolish things, you should do them when you still can and more importantly still want to. I read awhile back that, "a man is not old until regrets take the place of his dreams." As you get older, you might find it more reasonable to go out and buy a fishing pole rather than hiking poles. Many years ago, I had what we referred to as runner's mentality so I guess now I have hiker's mentality but I hope only a slight case. Tents were pitched that night at Lamberts Meadow Campsite.

Back on the trail at 3:30 AM, this night hiking seems to work for us. Reaching Daleville, Va. at 9 A.M., we checked into the Howard Johnson Express, showered, washed clothes then went for a lackluster breakfast at Bojangles. I then walked over to the Outdoor Trails, a full service outfitter and explained my foot problems to a sales lady. The first thing she did was measure my foot and found I needed a size 14. I have been wearing 12 or 13 since ninth grade but who was I to disagree with three toenails already gone and several blisters on each foot I was ready to try something new. She vanished for several minutes through a door leading to the back of the store and when she reappeared carried a box with more than a small amount of dust on it. She apologized, saying they were the only 14's in the store but for a hundred bucks I could have them. Sales people just see me coming. I laced them up and did two laps around the store before paying with the Visa card. Using the UPS Store two doors down I sent my heavy leather boots back to Georgia. It was a big chance to take but it worked out great, I will use them again next year.

Cricket, Ten-88, Mangy Mutt, and others are in town for the night. My daughter from Richmond, Va. and sister from the Upper Peninsula of Michigan tracked us down and stayed for a couple hours. This is a frequent happening on the trail, relatives or friends catching up with hikers for short visits.

Next morning we enjoyed a continental breakfast with a few of the older hikers. The young guys were long gone, looking for another 25 mile day, the rest of us seemed to realize the mountains would wait and our turn would come even after one more cup of coffee. Tom and I were back on the trail at 8 AM, about a mile out of town I noticed my new shoes, Montrail Hard Rocks matched my Go Light backpack perfectly, the fashion police would have nothing on me. The first two miles took us only 45 minutes; it is amazing what a good night's rest with good restaurant food does to your body, this in spite of the heavy food bags in our backpacks. As of Daleville, I lost eight pounds and Tom dropped 10. It's fun to watch other hikers in a grocery store, the product itself is of little consequence but the weight is paramount. It is hard not to purchase something if it weighs merely 3 ounces, cooks in three minutes and serves two, even if you did not like it the last time you bought it. The "serves two" part on the label is a deception as is the, "just like Mom used to make." It scarcely serves one and tastes mostly like white flour and pig fat but at the end of a hard days hike it's hot and something to look forward to. We hiked 14 miles this day and my knee was pain free as it would be for the rest of the journey.

The next day turned into 20 miler, the plan was to stop at the Bryant Ridge Shelter but a pack of Boy Scouts had laid claim to it by the time of our arrival. This is the shelter Cricket grilled fish for us but after a delicious meal with no tent sites available we moved half way up Floyd Mountain, about a thousand feet in less than two miles, not much fun at the conclusion of an already tough day. The foliage is at 80 percent and blocking the majority of views that might have been had earlier this spring but the rhododendrons are starting to blossom plus an assortment of small-multicolored ground flora keeps surprising us every day. Finding out Cricket was born in 1949, as Tom and I were; Tom declared the three of us, "The 49ers." It stuck the rest of the time we remained on the trail.

The following day was a 21 miler for a 55-mile total the last three days. Camp that night was at Matts Creek Shelter putting us only three miles from U.S. 501 and the James River. Tom has made arrangements with a shuttle service for transportation into Glasgow, Va., a six-mile ride. We survived a very heavy downpour last night, our tents held tight but all our gear is damp, it will be great to spend a night in town. The James River Foot Bridge is the longest foot use only bridge on the A.T. and dedicated to the memory of Bill Foot, a 1987 thru-hiker. Our driver, Ken Wallace, pulled up ten minutes after crossing the bridge at 7:30 A.M. and a few minutes later the town was ours. All ours as Tom and I were the only hikers in town. Glasgow is another small hiker town condensed with all services within half a mile. I forget the name of the motel we stayed at although it is the only one in town. The room assigned to us must have been designated the "hiker with wet dog room" as the aroma upon opening the door was about enough to have second thoughts. Of course, our option would have been to head back to the trail and sleep in a damp tent and that was not even discussed. There were two rooms, a sofa and T.V. in the front, a small bed, and another couch in the back room. After flipping a coin and winning I chose the bed. The bathroom came with its own kind of mold growing in the shower, the toilet seat was plastic and cracked so Tom walked a half mile to the Laundromat to take care of business rather than sit on it. I believe I had an off day and fortunately, it did not require a decision on my part. Out of curiosity, I picked up one of the couch cushions and found various food items, several toenails, a red balloon and 14 cents. Being a very frugal man, I was tempted but that 14 cents remains where I found it. Other than that our stay was great, the restaurant is part of the motel and the food was very good with a grocery store across the road and post office and laundry close at hand we enjoyed a relaxing day. The soreness in my knee was a past memory and my blistered feet were healing nicely. Life on the A.T. was good.

The next morning after western omelets and pancakes Ken chauffeured us back to the trail and it was a sweet trail at that, steep but well engineered with switchbacks and few rocks. Today's highlight was meeting 30 or 40 students from the Virginia Military Institute out on some sort of year-end exercises, a first-class group of young people. The trail talked us into 20 miles today. I guess our legs are becoming trail hardened as now 15 mile days are expected of them. While in Georgia to get in condition for this endeavor I rode a mountain bike and did a limited amount of hiking with a 30-pound pack. Tom, living in the land of perpetual snow, walked up and down his basement steps with a loaded pack. Yes, he said it was boring. Because of threatening rain, we spent the night in the shelter with three others at Brown Mill Creek. It was a frosty night and the day ahead would be an extremely tough one. With the temperature approximately 40 degrees or less and 30 mile an hour winds the rain started at 10 A.M. and persisted through-out the day. The 800 mile marker went by un-noticed, a milestone that normally would have meant pictures and high five's. Last night for supper, I consumed a bag of dehydrated chili and now I am paying the penalty. Gas, lots of gas being released while wearing rain gear is not a pleasant thing to tolerate, even with the stiff wind it lingers. A cold 16-mile day ended at 2:30 that afternoon at the Seeley-Woodworth Shelter. It took only minutes to change into dry clothing and crawl into our sleeping bags to regain the warmth our bodies very much needed. We were not in a great deal of danger however it certainly felt good to get out of the blustery weather. An hour later a small amount of hail fell and then at 5.P.M. the clouds went missing allowing the sun to drive some much needed BTU's our way. A line strung between trees and within an hour the majority of our damp gear was dry, a good thing given that it will be another cold night with another cold day to follow. I woke up around mid-night, cold and wishing I had my warmer sleeping bag but the darn thing weighs a pound more than this one so I wiggle into my rain gear hoping to stymie the heat loss and spend a fitful remainder of the night. This cold weather has caught me awfully ill-equipped. The next day, a 14 miler again proved cold and windy but dry and uneventful.

As I hike this twenty-second day on the trail, my thoughts are turning more to types of food that I miss. I am not underfed and in no danger of suffering from malnutrition but I have a longing for pizza, ice cream, and greasy fried chicken, the kind you get from the Colonel. I never eat that kind of chicken at home. However, there are other things on the menu; Tom has been to Russia twice so it is not uncommon to discover us sitting on a log in central Virginia eating Russian cheese and chocolate. In addition, my beef jerky is from Argentina, one pound for ten bucks; it would have cost me double that to make my own.

It was verified today that if your legs were made in 1949 twenty-two miles is about all you can expect from them. The strategy was to position ourselves five miles out of Rockfish Gap, Waynesboro, Va. There I would leave the trail for about four days while Tom and wife Lynn would hike approximately 100 miles in the Shenandoah National Park together. Our campground that night was the Paul C. Wolfe Shelter. I cooked some sort of noodle dish in my Jet Boil for supper and must not have done a good job cleaning it as in the morning I had a noodle swimming in my coffee. Only it was not a noodle, after spitting it out I realized that a slug had crawled into my cup sometime during the night. Another meaningless recollection that for some reason I will retain for years but what else do you acquire from a trip like this but memories; they need to be safeguarded, knowing that the memory is a fleeting thing and they will someday return to the earth with my ashes, so I write them down.

Hiking into Rockfish Gap in the morning, I munch on a granola bar, the last item in my food bag plus I ran out of toothpaste three days ago. This is cutting it close but the light backpack sure feels good. This morning I am having a political row with myself about Iraq, oil, and the desperate need of a strong third political party in this country. Some arguments I win, some I loose, some make little sense at all but the miles pass much faster if I think about things other than my next step. I am also getting a free botanical education of sorts as Tom has spent over 30 years with the U.S. Forest Service. He identifies birds I have not heard of, flowers that are new to my vocabulary and easily finds mushrooms that I walk past. His knowledge of such things makes the trip much more interesting, I just wish he could teach me to select a level tent site but in that respect both of us could do with a little help. Help came almost immediately as we reached the highway at Rockfish Gap scoring a ride the five miles into town. We checked into the Quality Inn, showered, did laundry and spent the rest of the day consuming as many calories as possible. Lynn and Sandy will be in town tomorrow. Tom and Lynn will stay on the trail, hiking to the northern end of the park while I will head east, spending time with family. The plan is for Tom and me to rendezvous in approximately eight days and continue on to southern Pennsylvania.

My itinerary off the trail included Mt. Vernon on the weekend, there were 50 tour buses parked in the lot but the lines moved quickly, it was worth the wait. Our first President had a great view of the Potomac River. We drove around Fredericksburg looking for a good restaurant and found many but not a place to park so it was back to our motel and a short walk across the street to a Golden Corral. It had ten tour buses already unloaded but again the lines moved right along and I enjoyed the all you can eat buffet. The next two days were spent in Richmond, Va. with daughter Bobbi and husband Ron. The time passed rapidly and soon it was Monday, May 19, time to return to the trail. Laden with a very heavy backpack at 12:30 that afternoon I was on my own, headed north. I stopped to register as I entered the Shenandoah National Park; it was like the Smokes all over again. They wanted to know where I would be at all times when inside the park. Having no idea as to my progress through the park I registered to stay at every shelter on the trail. Most other hikers did the same.

After walking 12 miles to the Wildcat Ridge area I stealth camped under a dreadfully rainy sky. All night it came down in buckets and it turned cold. Sometime during the night one of my rear tent stakes pulled loose allowing a good amount of water to drain off the fly and into my sleeping space. For just this once, I was fortunate that I selected yet another slopping tent site as the water stayed in the back of the tent, soaking only the foot end of my sleeping bag. Breaking camp in the rain is never an enjoyable thing, a hot meal is out of the question and a wet tent must add ten pounds to your pack weight. I walked for three hours in a downpour, arriving at Blackrock Hut around 9:30 A.M. where I cooked oatmeal for breakfast. There I talked to a 23 year Navy veteran, he told me of those 23 years 17 were served on a ship. The clouds started moving out and by midday, the heavens were filled with sunshine but a cool steady breeze persisted. I have noticed that the grass on the sides of the trail in the park has been mowed with some sort of mechanized piece of equipment. Who might they be trying to impress? By 4:30 that afternoon after 19 miles I arrived at the Pinefield Hut where I was able to dry my gear and prepare a very tasty supper. One good thing about a heavy food bag is the options it provides at mealtime but as always, I find myself eating first whatever weighs the most.

Another 20 miler the next day, the plan is to catch Tom and Lynn near the northern terminus of the park; they are doing ten to 14 mile days so it ought to work out. I start noticing many piles of bear crap on the trail and most other hikers have seen at least one of the critters. At a road crossing on Skyline Drive a sign tells me it takes 5 million steps to walk this trail in its entirety. That puts me within a couple hundred miles of doing half of them as I crossed the 900-mile marker today. Being alone I did not bother taking pictures. That night at Bearfence Mountain Hut the weather again turned cold, cold enough that at 1 A.M. it required the addition of rain gear to my already over dressed attire. It was late May; the people out here hiking were ready for some warmer temperatures. The mileage count for today will stop at 12 miles as this will put me at the Big Meadows Lodge for restaurant food and a visit to a well stocked bookstore at the Harry F. Byrd Sr. Visitor Center. Walking past the gas station my attention was drawn to the four dollar asking price for a gallon of no-lead. In a discussion with the attendant, a guy a little older than myself, we reminisced about gas being sold for 35 cents a gallon back in the day. Back when the music was worth listening to and you could ride around in your father's car all night for a dollars worth of petrol. And we had Hula Hoops rather than Game Boys. Growing up in the 60's was a great time to be young but now that I am pushing 60 I wonder if it is a good time to be old.

Moving forward up the trail I have been making a list of things that should be considered for next year's hike. Water proof and warm mittens head the list; the water repellent gloves I have are of little value once they stop repelling water and get wet. Also needed is a water proof stuff sack for my down sleeping bag, the one I have is nylon. More than likely the list will grow but for the most part my gear has served me well.

The best part of the day for me is at the conclusion of a hard days hike. After eating, while sitting on a rock or log to make an entry in my journal that will somehow make sense to me upon returning

90

home. Trying my hand at this writing trade has come slowly and poorly as I find it difficult to convey a sequence of events in a manner that is not only comprehensible but entertaining as well.

After three hours at the Big Meadows it is back on the trail, moving very slowly with belly full of restaurant food and I even bought a book to read at night. It's only three miles to Rock Spring Hut where I will spend a night that without doubt will be cold as per the weather station at the visitor's center, down into the 30's was the report. I became reacquainted with Half Time at the hut. He is a newly retired accountant from Florida attempting a thru-hike. The reasoning behind his trail name is that he, at 58 years of age is at the half way point in his life. I told him he was a very optimistic guy. He just chuckled. We hiked off and on together until Harpers Ferry and then I followed his progress when back home on Trailjournals.com. Shortly after crossing the Mason-Dixon Line he threw in the towel and headed home to Florida. Makes me wonder; does the trail smile a little with each victim it claims or is it remorseful that it is not more hospitable? The longer I stay on the trail the more it makes me realize that this is not so much a wilderness experience but a meeting of very interesting people and sometimes characters from all over the world. Half Time also advised me that the Park Service has 300 trail cameras mounted in the park to determine if Cougars are making a comeback in the area. I can only hope not.

It did get cold last night but I stayed surprisingly

warm with the help of a Heat Treat hand warmer placed in the bottom of my sleeping bag. Grabber Mycoal is the brand name and at less than a buck apiece we should have been using them all along. Walking fast early the next morning to stay warm, the trail in the park is like no other, well groomed and very gentle and sympathetic to an old man's legs. I would make a wager that more than one weekend vacationer having hiked the trails in the Shenandoah will go home planning a thru-hike the following year. They would be the ones that drop off before traversing the 75 miles in Georgia. Four miles up the trail put me at Skyland, yet another road crossing and another place to eat restaurant food. This is where Tom and I will reconnect and finish our push to the Mason-Dixon Line. It is a fine restaurant at Skyland with enormous windows overlooking the valley, a nice gathering place for vacationers. When a hiker walks in such as myself, 70 miles and five days without a shower you are escorted to the "hiker section," off to the side over by the kitchen door, a respectful distance from the higher tipping, better smelling tourists. Actually I am thankful they allowed me in at all. With the numerous opportunities to eat in the park I could be gaining weight.

It was good to be on the trail again with Tom, I went back to just hiking and left the planning to him. He had us scheduled to complete our hike three miles north of the Mason-Dixon Line on the first day of June. Thank goodness he also scheduled a "zero" day in Harpers Ferry so several 20 mile days became our mantra. The plan also included doing a "long one," a little north of here. The thinking was 30 miles would be a real test, it was, more about that in awhile. Thus far two bears have crossed my path but unlike other hikers I have not had any wood tics. It has been over 100 miles since my last shower so possibly that has something to do with it. We pushed on to Tom Floyd Wayside for the night, 952 miles from Springer Mountain in Georgia, another 100 miles and our hike will be over for this year. As I set my tent up that evening I observed two more bears within a hundred yards of my site, running full tilt up a hillside. Hopefully they kept going nevertheless we hung our food bags a little higher and I slept with a hiking pole by my side. The nights are now warm, extra clothes in the stuff sack mean a much larger and comfortable pillow. Little things mean so much. This hiking life is very simple but it can be hard. Attitude is important, as are dry socks, one can greatly affect the other.

Today the scuttlebutt on the trail is that Ted Kennedy has an inoperable brain tumor, last year it was the shootings at Virginia Tech and all I worry about is the next water supply. Life on the trail gives a person time to think about things like this but does it really matter?

Another 17 miles to the Bears Den Hostel and that means a much needed shower. It will be 8 days and 140 miles since I last got close to a bar of soap. It was an early start, 4:30 in the morning well before the birds would start singing and it was an effortless walk through the Sky Meadows State Park but then our

93

fortunes turned. The infamous Roller Coaster welcomed us back to the real world; fourteen miles of ten quick ascents and a like number of descents over an incredibly rocky and at times muddy trail. This is with-out a doubt some of the hardest hiking we have yet to experience. After the relatively easy 100 miles through the Shenandoah National Park, the Roller Coaster serves as a wake-up call and a step back into reality. This is the bona fide Appalachian Trail and if the first thousand miles has a soul, you will find it here. I believe if an atheist were fair warned of this stretch of trail he might ask for divine intervention before setting out. The Roller Coaster has me convinced that I would never try and persuade anyone into hiking this trail. If it is in your future you will as I did, discover it on your own. The trail is in charge here, it forced us into taking a break at Sam Moore Shelter for a snack and to rest our feet, which are very sore and tender from constantly stepping on rocks as they are many and they are sharp. I must give credit to our boots and shoes as they are of Herculean toughness to hold up for even a short distance. Three miles later a hostel never looked so good, the Bears Den, by far the finest hostel thus far on the trail. For 25 bucks, you get a clean bunk, shower, laundry, kitchen privileges, a frozen pizza, and a pint of Ben and Jerry's Ice Cream. A confession here, this is the first occasion in my 58 years that I have eaten Ben and Jerry's Ice cream, it is incredibly first-class. An extra bonus was being reunited with Ten 88; we lost contact with him two weeks ago but he was there and welcomed us in. It was a tough day, bedtime came early, by eight that evening it was lights out. Our 1949 model bladders seem to fill up around 4 A.M. Not wanting to rouse the rest of the crew we snuck outside and cooked breakfast on a picnic table under the gazebo. It was 20 miles to Harpers Ferry but still having three hills of the Roller Coaster to conquer it was at a measured pace hiking out of the Bears Den. At 6:30 that morning our goodbyes were said to Virginia and West Virginia welcomed us with a spectacular sunrise. This was an enormous psychological boost; 550 miles in the Commonwealth of Virginia was now behind us. It is a great state with extremely friendly people but the magnitude of it made me happy that it was in my rear view mirror. This border crossing in particular required high-fives and many pictures. Once off the Roller Coaster the trail returned to somewhat normal if there is such a thing out here. We stopped at David Lesser Shelter for a break and Tenderfoot was there to greet us. It is always good to see old friends. That is a strange remark. I have known him only a few weeks but refer to him as an old friend. Hiker mentality? A short distance later the one thousand mile marker from Springer Mountain appears, a huge highlight of the excursion and I think it may have triggered some emotions with us as we now include in our conversations plans of returning home.

By mid-afternoon, we crossed the Shenandoah River and what a river it is, wide and shallow with rapids both up and down stream; it makes an immense first impression. While still on the trail near Harpers Ferry a Trail Angel met and invited us to a cookout at

95

his home right next to the Appalachian Trail Conservancy. Even before finding a room or taking a shower a trail angel treated us to hamburgers, hotdogs, and a host of cold dishes that were devoured without regard to any manners that may have been learned years before. I cannot remember the guys name but he does this all the time and wants nothing in return. The General and Twenty Blisters joined us for the feast as well. The General, from England was attempting his second thru hike. I asked him what would make him do such a thing twice, he replied, "The answer will be found on the trail." I left it go at that. He was a tall powerfully built guy and I would put my money on his quest of a second through hike without problem.

Harpers Ferry with all its historic grandeur is not an inexpensive place to take a zero day but for that very reason, its historic significance we did just that. After thanking our un-named Trail Angel, Tom and I walked up and then down a steep hill to the Comfort Inn and booked two nights. Later that day with excellent cell service, I made phone calls to Michigan, Virginia, and Georgia. Sandy brought me up to date on my reservations with Amtrak for my return trip to Georgia.

Our thirty-seventh day on the trail was spent touring Harpers Ferry, the town is small and the restaurants are within easy walking distance. It seemed the whole gang was here, Pilgrim, a minister from Kansas City, Jack Frost from Arizona, Tenderfoot from South Carolina, Ten 88 from New Jersey, and Nebo from Alabama. All thru hikers with the exception of Nebo who was leaving the trail at this point. Our zero day was spent at the A.T. Conservancy, a small but well stocked outfitter, the train station, some of the historic buildings and as before mentioned, eating massive amounts of restaurant food. The talk even turned of ways to keep from regaining the weight lost in the last six weeks, having each dropped close to 15 pounds off bodies that were not exactly corpulent to begin with. I'm doubtful the weight will stay off but I do feel better weighing 185 pounds rather than 205. Also, after 80 days and a thousand miles of hiking my off trail eating habits have improved measurably having restricted the amount of sugar while increasing more nutritious types of food.

Our short stay in Harpers Ferry reinvigorated our bodies but may have had a negative effect on our intellect. One of us, I will not say who but it was not me came up with the suggestion of doing a long one the first day out of town. Some of the younger hikers do the "four state challenge," starting just inside the Virginia border they then cover West Virginia, Maryland and into Pennsylvania for a total of well over 40 miles in a 24 hour period. Such an undertaking would be out of the question for us old gray beards but attempting to do 30 miles in a 24 hour stretch verifies that wisdom is definitely a slow ripening fruit. We checked out of the Comfort Inn at 4 A.M. and walked for three hours before taking a break. Pusher, a young man from New England passed by in an attempt at the four state challenge. We wished him well and he the same to us on our pursuit of 30. Late that afternoon, after 27 miles I sat on a log at the Pogo Memorial Campsite. I was tired and every bone in my body implored me to pitch my tent and crawl into my sleeping bag without further a due. Tom joined me a few minutes later, physically in the same shape but with a brighter mental outlook. We ate cheese and crackers, looked and re-looked at the maps and somehow mustered the strength to move on to the Ensign Cowall Shelter for a total of 32 miles in about 15 hours of hiking. On arrival I quickly cooked something to eat and then slept as sound as I have in the last six weeks.

Surprisingly it was a 5:30 wakeup the next morning and not feeling all that bad. Today will be our final day on the trail until next year and with only 13 miles to go this hike will be over shortly after noon. Later that morning we found Pusher at his campsite just north of the Mason Dixon line. It took him less than 22 hours to complete the four state challenge. This of course called for another round of congratulations and picture taking. At 30 minutes past noon on the first day of June, 2008 the trail that had been our home for the last six weeks ended. As planned, Tom's truck sat there waiting and it was a short drive back to Harpers Ferry. I checked into the local hostel as my train reservations were for the following day, Tom headed back to Michigan. How quickly it all ended but not before plans were discussed for next year's expedition. That afternoon while sitting on the steps outside the hostile I casually looked through a handful of coins and of all things found a

1949 nickel. I guess the Forty-Niners are for real, I saved it.

I slept poorly that night as the hostel is located only a quarter mile from the railroad tracks and trains seemed to run every hour or so. Not wanting to miss my ride into Washington D.C. for my connection to Atlanta I arrived at the train station at 11:30 A.M. for a 12:15 P.M. departure. How foolish of me, the darn thing finally made an appearance at 2:45, two and a half hours late. Lucky for me my departure out of D.C. was scheduled for 6 P.M. so I had time to play with. The ride to Atlanta was uneventful but very long, 14 hours. It was good to be home.

CHAPTER THREE

AUGUST 8 2009

North of Harpers Ferry to New York 22

Of Rocks and Deli's

May 3, 2009, Ironmasters Mansion Hostel, just south of the entrance to Pine Grove Furnace State Park, Pennsylvania. We made it, Tom and me, after a 4 A.M. departure, driving 13 hours from Brimley, Michigan south through the Lower Peninsula and then catching every tollbooth Ohio and Pennsylvania could throw at us. The plan was to leave Tom's truck here and return via Amtrak at the conclusion of our hike.

I was worried, possibly even overly concerned. According to CNN, the Swine Flu was sweeping the country, even the world. Our newly elected Vice-President, Joe Biden warned us against riding on airplanes, sub-ways and any other type of mass transit and to avoid crowds in general while President Obama advised us to wash our hands. I did everything that was asked with one exception, I along with 5,000 others participated in the graduation ceremony at Lake Superior State University as my youngest nephew picked up a well-deserved degree. I really wasn't paying much attention other than if I heard one person cough I was out of there, hell bent on avoiding this deadly infection that already killed one person in Texas. With an incubation period of three to seven days I had no desire to become sick within the first week of the hike. I believe Dana also had reservations about this as he was leavening on a 60-day kayak adventure within the week. I heard no one sneeze or cough but I held my breath for the five minutes it took to walk out of the auditorium. My face was turning blue as I made the last few steps towards the car.

It was an 800-mile drive with the intention of hiking 400, some of it in the rain and on very slippery rocks. We would be hot, cold, wet and occasionally dry but rarely hungry. Long distance hikers call this having fun. I can only imagine the pizza and jelly filled donuts I could be buying with the money this trip is costing.

I now sit in the Earl Shaffer Memorial Dining Hall at the hostel. Earl was the first thru hiker, way back in 1948 using gear he acquired while in the Army. The "Crazy One" they called him. Wearing worn boots, he carried neither stove nor tent. Earl hiked it again in 1965 and again in 1998 at age 79, marking his fiftieth anniversary of his first hike. The gear utilized today gives us an undisputable advantage over not only the pioneers of the trail but of hikers from only a few years past.

For 25 bucks a bunk is provided, a shower, and kitchen privileges. As hostels go this one is not so bad. It was built in 1827 and served as a station on the Underground Railroad, even has a secret room, I saw it.

This evening we visited with two other hikers and a New York City guy here gathering information on the Civil War. Being only 25 miles from Gettysburg the hostel serves as a great place to stay for folks doing Civil War research. When this hike is over the plan is to spend a day in the Big Apple so we peppered our new acquaintance with questions. What are the chances of being mugged? Is it expensive to eat in a restaurant? What about the sub-way? I believe he was amused and had us figured for what we are; two small town boys on our first trip to the big city. The two of us also engaged in a lengthy conversation about the JFK assassination. He adamantly believes in the conspiracy theory and me the premise of the single shooter. He thought the Warren Commission was a cover up and even hinted that perhaps Vice President Johnson or the mafia may have been party to the assassination. An interesting discussion about something that happened when I was 14 years old, the guy from New York had not yet been born. The evening passed quickly and it was soon bedtime, it was about 8:30.

Morning came early. A quick breakfast and a short wait for Roger, Tom's former boss during his years with the U.S. Forest Service. Conveniently for us, Roger lived in the vicinity and would shuttle us approximately 35 miles south to Pennsylvania highway 16, last year's stopping point. The plan was to hike back to this hostel in two days as the trail ran within yards of the building and spend the night before moving on. Thirty-five miles in the first two days would be very aggressive for a couple of guys born in 1949 but Mother Nature would provide incentive. It was raining when Roger took our pictures at 9:30 that morning and it continued to either drizzle or rain cats and dog's all day long, and it was cold, maybe 40 degrees. So much fun and only our first day.

Again, a 20-mile day in the books had us staggering, wet and tired into Quarry Gap Shelter at 6:30 that evening. The first 2.4 miles were covered in 45 minutes showing that adrenalin still affects the bodies of men born in the first half of the last century. Three years ago when I initially started this quest, discipline was the rule of the day. Justin and I hiked 50 minutes at a slow pace and rested for ten minutes while eating a high-energy granola bar. The adopted strategy now seems that we walk to the point of exhaustion and then walk a few more miles. Of course my brain tells me to keep hiking but my body is saying something like, "wait a second, this needs to be discussed." This first day turned out to be much longer than planned and more miserable than imagined but setting a tent up in the rain is one of my least favorite things so we soldiered on to the shelter. There we spent the night with K.Z. and The Fence Man, both from Albuquerque, New Mexico and Jake, a 64-year-old lean mean hiking machine from north Georgia. I asked Fence Man, at least 60 years old if he was a thru-hiker,

"Yep" he replied, "I could be through any day now". He and K.Z. hiked a thousand miles last year and were back to finish the job. Parts of the next three weeks would be spent with these guys. I cannot explain how quickly friendships develop on the trail. Unfortunately, they can evaporate just as fast. It was a good group of guys with many sunsets in our pasts and eagerly treating each sunrise as it could be our last.

Day two the rain stopped but the trail was a mess, very muddy, slippery and in places like a small stream, every drop of water attempting and mostly succeeding to penetrate our hundred dollar Gore-tex hiking shoes. Later in the day, the five of us regrouped at the Birch Run Shelter for a short rest and bite to eat. I believe K.Z. was the youngest of the group at 56. There we sat with boots and socks off trying to dry up a little in the paltry rays of sunshine provided by the sun god. After a short time, a youthful college student walked in to join us. I am sure he thought he walked into a convalescent home of some sort, we were a sorry looking bunch. The log registered 17 more miles that day, returning to the Iron Masters Hostel for a greatly appreciated hot shower and a chance to dry our gear. Still having a few hours of daylight we jumped in Tom's truck and headed to town for a not so tasty hamburger at Jo's Home Cooking. Having spent only two days on the trail, I am still particular about our choice of food. Three weeks later that same burger would have been considered first rate. This short excursion also included a quick tour of the Gettysburg Battlefield. If you stayed there long enough and listened close enough, I believe the sounds that dying men make could still be heard. The picture in my head was not good, 150 years later we carry on like absolutely nothing has been learned.

The next day of our hike started at 6:30 under cloudy skies but warm temperatures. After only an hour, we reached the official but not entirely accurate halfway point on the trail. Pictures were taken in mass; the sign told us it was 1,085 miles from our goal, Mt. Katahdin, Maine.

The knee that bothered me so much last year was again talking to me but in a lesser way. I found my patella knee band at the bottom of my pack and it seemed to do the trick as within a mile the pain vanished but I continued to wear it for the duration of the journey. Soon other problems came our way; the infamously legendary rocks of Pennsylvania were starting to show their ugly head. Every book that has ever been penned regarding the A.T. squanders a paragraph or two and sometimes a full page describing these rocks. I would be calling them everything but rocks before completing the state of Pennsylvania. I will keep my complaints and depiction short. They are small like baseballs, large like Cadillac's, and everything in-between, they are pointed and very sharp and they are round and they are many. They are imbedded in the ground and they are loose, waiting for a miss-aligned step to turn your ankle and if possible on a good day break your leg. They are bothersome at best, never allowing a hiker to hit a good stride. I complained for the duration while in Pennsylvania about the rocks as they take so much away from the hike but yet they are the trail and they are part of the deal.

Fortunately, the hiking is relatively flat and the state of Pennsylvania was put to bed in 13 days of rather aggressive hiking. Our feet were very tender upon completion, like someone took one of those old-fashioned metal meat-tenderizing hammers and beat the crap out of them like they were a cheap flank steak. Such is the trail in Pennsylvania; it was only to get worse as we progressed north.

The leaves are well budded out on the trees and we are surprised but pleased at the lack of mosquito's or sand flies. I picked ramps, or leaks along the trail this afternoon to mix with mashed potatoes tonight. We did a rather strenuous climb late in the day along with a high water river crossing before setting up camp at the Alec Kennedy Shelter. Fence Man, K. Z. and Jake joined us. The five of us enjoyed the chitchat you would expect from five senior citizens sitting in a shelter on the Appalachian Trail in southern Pennsylvania.

The plan on day four was to hike 18 miles to the Darlington Shelter but common sense and a little bit of lethargy interrupted the schedule. A hard rain last night left the trail muddy and the rocks slippery. We were motivated by our guidebooks information that four miles up the trail lay Boiling Springs, the five of us planned to meet at Anile's for a big blueberry pancake breakfast. Hard luck would be our companion this wet and foggy morning as to our dismay the restaurant was closed, out of business. The next best thing was a corner Getty Mart gas station. Pancakes and hot strong coffee was the dream, the reality was Gatorade and hotdogs off the rotisserie. I am certain the one I picked had spun around on the thing for at least three days. Tom read the guidebook as I finished licking ketchup off my fingers. "Look here," he let me see the book. Eight miles north, we would cross highway 11 and therein lay the Middlesex Diner. If not breakfast why not dinner? within four hours it would be restaurant food of one sort or another. We left Boiling Springs high stepping with smiles on our faces.

     The sign in front of the restaurant said something like "good food and plenty of it," it was so right, and I highly recommend it. After eating, our ambition was nowhere to be found and the thought of hiking another six miles vanished. Right across busy highway 11 stood a Super 8 Motel with a ten percent hiker discount. That night would be spent between warm clean sheets watching cable T.V. Life was good.

     At about 7:30 sleep came easy but by 3:30 the next morning it was all over, time to start moving. It was a short walk across highway 11 to the 24-hour Diner for more pancakes than anyone should ever eat. By 4:30, it was back on the dew-covered trail with the aid of headlights. As the sun made its way over the horizon, I met a south bounder from Harrisburg, Pa. running the trail as a workout for a 100-mile ultra-marathon he would participate in later this month. Apparently, we were also moving at a good pace as at noon we walked into Duncannon, Pa. 17.7 miles in seven and a half hours. Today gives the impression that our hiking legs are starting to come around. The mutual feeling is that several more miles could have been logged. We headed straight to the famous, at least to us hikers, Doyle Hotel. Built by the Anheuser-Busch Company years ago, the hotel is a landmark not to be missed by hikers in the area. The place has fallen on hard times but it appears the present owners, Pat and Vicky Kelly are making an attempt at restoration. From what I have learned it is one of seven hotels built by the beer company following World War I, only two continue to exist. For 30 bucks, we got a room with two beds on the top floor, use of the washing machine and dryer, and a much appreciated hot shower in the bath three doors down the hall from our room. I might add that we enjoyed some of the finest food on the trail at the Doyle. We also had the good fortune to spend more time with Jake as he strolled in later that afternoon.

Next day after a quick breakfast, it was back on the trail by 6 A.M. I started thinking about a story I read yesterday in the local paper about the passing of Jack Kemp, former quarterback for the Buffalo Bills and Congressman from New York plus Bob Dole's vice presidential running mate. He was described as a bleeding heart conservative. Rest in peace Jack Kemp. My thoughts almost immediately returned to the business at hand as the trail quickly presented us with a thousand foot climb spread over approximately two miles.

This is the first year I have been adding supplements to my drinking water such as Gatorade and PowerAde. I am not sure they do much good other than change the taste of the water.

Today I passed a turtle on the trail, he was headed north, I wished him luck and speculated on the amount of time it would take him to summit Katahdin? A little later, a black snake laying on the trail scared the heck out of me. Around noon, I met a south bounder and when asked how far he was going he quickly responded, "As far as I can make it." "Good attitude," I replied.

It seems today is the day for seeing things on the trail other than hikers. After 26 hard miles, it was well past the time to start looking for a place to tent. I have never seen or heard a rattlesnake before but 30 feet away I knew exactly what lay on the trail ahead. He was big, like my wrist. I stopped so suddenly Tom walked into me. Tom could see him but because of a hearing problem could not hear him. Not a good situation for Tom or the snake. I pitched a handful of small rocks and sticks at our distraction but he made no effort to abandon his place on the trail. I guess he figured he was there first, this was his home and he was willing to defend it. We were fine with that and made a very large detour through a rhododendron thicket before returning to the trail about 40 feet north of the big guy protecting his turf. After a few pictures, at distance, and a short discussion, we were in complete compliance with the plan of not camping anywhere near this area. After a quick glance at the map, our only choice was to carry on another three miles to the Rausch Gap Shelter for a total of almost 29 miles that day. After a short break and dumping of surplus water to lighten our loads fear and adrenalin delivered us to the shelter just as day turned to night. Three other hikers were already in attendance but they made room for us and the best part is I was so drained I did not think of the snake again until the next day. After a hastily prepared dinner, it was lights out at 9 P.M.

It was 7 A.M. before hitting the trail in the morning, late for us but I speculate we are feeling the end product of the extended journey yesterday. I now have small blisters on the balls of both feet and also on my little toe on my left foot. This is the third year with blisters on that toe, I thought of having it cut off but a guy on Wikipedia claimed I would start walking around in circles. What would the civilized world do without Wikipedia?

Our seventh day of hiking ended at the 501 Shelter giving us 126 miles for an 18 mile average, much more aggressive than planned. This is a great shelter; it has four walls and a roof with a giant skylight, 12 individual bunks and is close enough to town that the pizza man delivers. In an unconventional move, we declined the pizza and ate provisions out of our packs for the sole purpose of shedding a few ounces. I hit the bunk at 7 P.M. and slept soundly until six the next morning, 11 hours of much needed rest.

Back on the trail this morning at one of many vistas I noticed a very neat looking farm with the customary red barn, white clapboard house, plowed patchwork fields along with many head of cattle of one sort or another. It made me think of President Eisenhower's farm but I knew little about it other than it was in this state somewhere. After a quick visit to Google I now know his farm is adjacent the Gettysburg Battlefield. We were nearby and did not even know it.

This is our eighth day hiking and the rocks have intensified, I'm thinking maybe the farmers down in the valley hauled them up here when they cleared their fields years ago. On the other hand, maybe on the seventh day God chuckled and chucked rocks at Pennsylvania. Again, "death by a thousand cuts" comes to mind, a form of punishment dished out by the Imperial Chinese for the worst of crimes committed. Are we being punished by the trail? My feet would say yes. I have them covered with duck tape, it helps a little. I soon came across a monument denoting an outpost setup during the French and Indian Wars. It makes me wonder if they rode horses up here. It is hard enough to find a suitable place for my two feet let alone a horse with four. God bless the horses.

We stopped at the Eagles Nest Shelter for a short break and to cook supper before moving on an additional three miles. Eventually level ground appeared allowing us to pitch our tents for the first time. Rocky terrain, wet weather, mostly vacant shelters and of course the fear of snakes had us utilizing the shelters to this point.

Of course, the rain came last night and that means a wet pack-up but it is only five miles to Port Clinton where our first mail drop awaits us. Once in town it was a short walk to an outfitter whose name I do not recall and retrieved the care packages we sent to ourselves two weeks ago. It was another mile to the only restaurant in town that served breakfast but luck was a lady this morning. In fact two of them. In a van came Fence Man and K Z's support team, having recently dropped the guys off to do a slack pack. Like good trail angels, they offered a ride and we begged them to come in for coffee while we ate, not so much for company but for a return ride to the trail. I am positive they were aware of our motive. They agreed. Thank you ladies.

Back on the trail, it was less than another mile to high-way 61 where we timidly stuck our thumb in the air merely to witness car after car pass us by. Our feet were hurting and my shoes were falling apart faster than I could Shoe Goo them together but the one mile march to the Microtel Inn would be worth every last step. Our gear needed to be dried and Tom was having a little problem with hemorrhoids. Having no Preparation-H he did the next best thing an innovative fellow could do, he used his Chap Stick. He said it came down to taking care of one end or the other. There was also a Cabela's a short distance away, plus a Cracker Barrel restaurant. We visited both, the latter with our old friend Jake whom we by chance bumped into in the motel lobby. Although Jake is a little older than Tom and I, we made him an honorary member of the Forty-Niners. After telling him that at age 65 he was an inspiration to the rest of us hikers he started laughing, telling us that when people start saying you are an inspiration and call you sir it is just about the end of the line. Walking across the parking lot the next morning on the way back to the trail we noticed the van from

New Mexico, it would be our last contact with Fence Man and K Z. I hope they make it to Katahdin.

Road walking back to the trail required us to cross a bridge that was under repair, about a 300 footer. Before setting foot on the bridge, the cockiest little tobacco chewing straw boss you can imagine made it clear that our presence would not be tolerated on his jobsite. I am sure he had a staring roll in the old movie "Deliverance". He threatened to call the State Police if we chose to do so. Now I am the type that if there alone I would have taken my pack off and wrestled with the little shit-head. I wisely followed Tom's lead and continued walking, all the while waiting for a ball peen hammer to hit me in the back of my head. He had the disposition of the rattlesnake but with less diplomatic characteristics. Jake caught up with us later that day and enlightened us about a like adventure on the bridge.

Right after that escapade, it was back on the trail and climbing a seven hundred footer up the side of an un-named mountain. Time to bitch about the trail again. I am starting to realize that my Montrail Hard Rocks are no match for the rocks on this part of the trail. Chunks the size of nickels are falling off the bottoms of my shoes but perhaps these rocks serve a purpose. If nothing else, they provide an anchor to slow an already aggressive pace. As we enter our final days in Pennsylvania and putting it in perspective, it is not an enjoyable state to hike. The locals are friendly and the re-supply points are numerous along with well maintained shelters and beautiful vistas however thus far it is the last section of the trail I would return to hike again. On a lighter note, I smile when I think what "Katz" of Bill Bryson's "Walk in the Woods" would have articulated about these blessed rocks. I promise, no more bad mouthing the rocks.

Hikers are a work in contradiction, walking 20 or more miles a day and pleased to do it. Arriving at a shelter after a hard day only to discover the water source is two tenths of a mile down a blue blaze trail. Well the indignity of it all. What were they thinking? Another two tenths? Off the trail? Makes ya want to write a letter or at least make a phone call. I am bushed and I prefer the water to be right in front of the shelter. It's just a hiker's mentality, certainly not a discredit to all the volunteers that make this possible, without them this trail would not survive and I thank everyone that ever worked even an hour on it.

A 22 mile hike today and the night was spent at the Allentown Hiking Shelter with the other 49er, Jake.

The next morning rain made breakfast a hurried ordeal and it continued most of the day causing some concern as we crossed an area described in the guide book as, "The Cliffs, Knife Edge." The plan is to hike 17 miles and hitch a ride into Lehigh Gap and spend the night at "Fine Lodging." And fine it was, after a phone call from the trail, Ira Fine, proprietor of Fine Lodging picked us up at the road crossing, Pa. 873 in a 1970's something woody station wagon. It was a perfect car for transporting hikers, big and roomy and all the damage that could be done to the interior was already completed. The hotel was huge; three stories if I remember right and the floors were incredibly un-level. The aroma upon entering the lobby would suggest that of a wet dog. Or perhaps that of a whole sled dog team over a long period of time; it was very hard to get used to. We paid 44 bucks for a room with two beds and received a room with one bed and a mattress on the floor. There were two TV's, the second one an old tube type Zenith that did not work but apparently, Ira had no impulse to throw it out. The bathroom down the hall was not so bad but I doubt my wife Sandy would stay here. To be fair, Ira is an ok guy, he picked us up the next morning and dropped us off back at the trail, not bad for 22 dollars each. He left us with a handful of his business cards to pass out on the trail. They read, "Fine Lodging, clean, safe, tastefully furnished rooms and Apts. for quiet, refined individuals." Ira is one of those guys you just have to love.

The first trail mile out of Lehigh Gap included a thousand foot climb on exposed rock that was very challenging and at times even a little unnerving. It took us a full hour to reach the summit. According to our guide book there would be no water on the trail for the next 16 miles compelling us to hike with full water bottles. We reached the Leroy Smith Shelter in the early afternoon where two college students were already camping. Despite the light rain, the four of us slept dry and sound in the shelter built for eight but it was back on the trail at 4:30 A.M. with a long hard twenty mile day ahead of us. Later that day in an extremely rocky area, we met a large group of Boy Scouts out for a day hike. One of the more talkative kids asked where I was from, I told him "Michigan."

He replied, "Oh, so your just here for the fun of it." I did not have an answer for him.

Another 20-mile day took us to Pennsylvania 611/Delaware Water Gap in about ten hours, walking into the Presbyterian Church of the Mountain Hostel at 2:30 P.M. We met Tennessee there, a retired schoolteacher from the state he took his trail name from. It is a free hostel, asking for a donation only if you are able.

The next day would be our last full one in Pennsylvania. Anytime you put a state in the rear view mirror, it is a good psychological feeling and with Pennsylvania I find that particularly accurate but shortly the bears of New Jersey will be ours to contend with. It is reported that Jersey has more bears per square mile than any other state. Rather than hanging bear bags at night all the shelters in this area had large metal boxes for us to store our food bags while sleeping. Pennsylvania's 226 miles were covered in 13 days for an average of 17 and a half miles a day. The trail in this state to me is a trail of contradictions. The footpath itself I can find few words of admiration but the re-supply opportunity's and chances to eat restaurant food have been unmatched thus far. Then again, my feet are very tender and my shoes are just about shot. I am looking forward to New Jersey.

Today the trail will take us across the Delaware River into New Jersey and out of Pennsylvania for a total of only ten miles to the Mohican Outdoor Center. It is operated by the Appalachian Mountain Club as a retreat center. Very nice semi-private rooms with kitchen privileges and showers for about 25 bucks. A good deal, Sandy would stay here. I need a short day if for nothing else preventive medicine. Day after day, the trail beats me up, it lets me climb a thousand footer but it extracts a little something from me. It lets me think I am winning but after several days of hard hiking, it is easy to understand who will be the winner without a short or even a zero day.

May 17th, day 15 on the trail started out at a cool 40 degrees but we later find out it is snowing in Michigan. So far the trail in New Jersey somewhat resembles that of Pennsylvania with long stretches of rocks but our hopes of a smoother trail will eventually come true.

Tonight our tents were pitched at Glen Anderson Shelter and I dressed heavily before crawling into my sleeping bag as the weatherman predicted below freezing temperatures. He was wrong and I am grateful. A light rain fell during the night mixed with a mild wind that caused a small amount of water to enter my tent. It seems the rain fly should be about three inches longer at the foot end. I have made a note of this and will try to modify the fly for next year as this has happened before.

Day 16 and 17 entailed a little over 37 miles taking a big bite out of the 72 miles of trail in New Jersey. Tom and I were both surprised at how heavily forested this state is. Smoke stacks and heavy traffic were expected but pleasant vistas and eventually a very nice trail made this state one of my favorites. It took us ten quick miles to High Point State Park where the last of our mail drops were waiting. It was a beautiful fall day to sit on the picnic table and cook up a delicious meal of salmon and mashed potatoes with chicken gravy. Hiking out of the park with full bellies and heavy packs made for slow going, the mail drops are always nice but the extra weight makes me wonder if I really need it all. After another eight miles, we hit Lott Road and walked a half mile into Unionville N.Y. At the post office, I mailed home 15 ounces of un-needed stuff, mostly clothes. It is a psychological happening when any hiker can do that, almost a full pound. Unionville is a hiker friendly town with free tenting with water and toilet facilities located at the Unionville Memorial Park. But wait a second; Unionville has even better to offer. The Mayor's House, home of the former mayor, Dick, his sidekick Butch, and the crabby looking but mostly gracious Bill, a rejuvenated 81 year old Korean War Veteran who makes things happen. A note posted at the park with a phone number informed us that the mayor would not only put us up for the night but also feed us supper and breakfast, wash our clothes, let us shower and all for free. There is a donation cup located in the kitchen and contributions were made. Several very comfortable bunks in the basement along with a delicious meal cooked up by Bill who spent his working life as a matradee at a very exclusive hotel. The next morning we hiked out heavy with water as the guide book informed us of little or none on today's trail. A slight tenth of a mile diversion led the way to Heaven Hill Farm where milk shakes and ice cream cones were enjoyed by Tom, myself and a few others. Tennessee was also there but this would be our last meeting as he planned on taking the rest of the day off. It was a satisfying way to spend an hour on a warm sun filled afternoon. After a short discussion, the decision was made to end the hike early, by several days. The logic being to assure enough miles remaining that would warrant two more years of hiking. It was that easy, when we hit N.Y. 22, ironically on our twenty-second day of hiking, it would be our last, leaving us with about 750 miles for the following two years. The miles this year went by much faster than I believed could happen. The first two years of this adventure saw us averaging 13 to 14 miles a day but with the relatively flat trail in Pennsylvania and easy going in New Jersey and New York, we are running way ahead of schedule. Tom and I are both former high school milers and I am convinced when the hike starts in the morning somewhere in the back of our minds a starter's gun is fired, and the race begins.

That night was spent tenting at the Wawayanda Shelter with several other section hikers. A nice shelter but the water supply is about half a mile away. One particular hiker, I forget his name was a 71 year old retired school teacher that attempted a thru-hike last year but became sick on the trail, forcing him to abandon his dream of completing the journey in one year. He was back with thoughts of finishing this year. It turned out to be perhaps the warmest night thus far, making my sleeping bag just another layer between my body and the ground. At 4:30 A.M. after the customary coffee and oatmeal breakfast, I followed Tom on the trail to New York. After two hours, it was photo and high-five time at the state line. Fifteen minutes later off to the east I vaguely made out the sky line of New York City. A planned lunch break 12 miles into the day at the Wildcat Shelter re-energized our legs but with ten more to go some tough hiking remained. The stretch between West Mombasha Road and New York 17 is definitely the most difficult of this year's hike. We met south bound hiker Dinosaur, a 60 year old from Florida not knowing for sure how long he would stay on the trail. He had two full cartons of cigarettes in his pack, telling us that the darn things cost almost 80 dollars a carton in New York. Once at N.Y. 17 a two mile road walk remained to the Tuxedo Motel in Southfields, N.Y. Despite the warning in the guidebook about hikers being cited we tried hitching but had no luck. Other than being out of the way the Tuxedo Motel is an ok place to spend the night. It offered the choice of three different restaurants that delivered and I believe we picked Italian. More pasta.

Knowing our time on the trail was short, probably four days, the next morning we mailed home every piece of non- essential and even some essential gear to help reduce pack weight. Both packs were lightened by over four pounds. I'll keep my fingers crossed and hope to stay warm and dry as I no longer have extra clothing but the 25 pound pack sure is nice. I will also limit my phone calls as I have sent my charger home saving another ounce and a half. After a quick stop at a deli for bagels and coffee and then we begged a ride back to the trail with a local guy that seemed not real sure that he wanted to do this. Two car miles later and another 20 mile hiking day began. The mosquitoes are becoming a real problem and the heat is rising but after about five miles I get the crazy idea in my head that I should try and run the Boston Marathon or ride my bike cross country. It is warm but not so warm that it should affect my thinking in any way so I will just let it pass, for now. I can see Sandy's eyes rolling to the back of her head when she reads this.

By two that afternoon, I finished my sixth 20 ounce bottle of water. Normally not something worth keeping track of but for some reason today I did, at least until then. I have no idea how much I consumed after that. At 7:30, we crossed the Hudson River and an hour later arrived at the Hemlock Springs Campsite where head lights were required to set up the tents and cook supper. It was a very hot humid night but sleep came easy and stayed that way until six the following morning.

It was only four miles the next day to U.S. 9 and a stop for coffee and bagels. Next year when the hiking returns to a more conventional form, I sure will miss the convenience of all the road crossings. It took us eight hours to walk 16 miles today and another mile to Clarence Fahnestock State Park where lot number three became our home for the night, the most un-level tent site in the whole world. I think I have said that before and it was free so maybe I should stop complaining.

Next day was a tough 16 miler under very cloudy skies but we reached Morgan Stewart Shelter before

121

the rains came down. When she let loose, she came hard and fast with high wind and lightning, a small amount of water again entered my tent at the foot end. Word on the trail the next day is that four hikers were struck by lightning at another shelter.

Our last day of hiking will be short, about 11 trail miles to N.Y. 22 but another 2.6 miles of road walk to the Dutchess Motor Lodge. This particular place was picked as our destination because of its location in regards to the New York City commuter train. The plan is to spend the night at the Dutchess and catch the Metro North train into New York City the next day. Our hike ended this year at 11:45 A.M. as the Forty-Niners stepped off the trail and onto pavement for a long walk to the motel where we enjoyed showers, washed clothes and of course ate restaurant food. Early the next morning it was off to catch the 5:28 train into the city. It cost 35 bucks for round trip tickets and within 90 minutes the train rolled into Grand Central Station where bagels and coffee made for a great breakfast. From there, after purchasing all day sub-way tickets and promptly boarding the wrong train our day in New York City was underway. The idea was to head south down by the financial district but after a short while Tom realized the train was going north. Again, he proved to be not only a master on the A.T. but also on the asphalt and concrete trails of this huge city. Left to myself I probably would have ridden that train north until they kicked me off. Once on the south bound train we were soon on Wall Street. After taking only one picture of the New York Stock Exchange the battery's in my camera gave up the ghost, I purchased two double AA's from a street vendor for $4.50. No Wal-Mart available. Right across the street is a large statue of George Washington as this is the place he was sworn in as our first president. After more pictures, it was off to find "the bull." Below is a brief description, barrowed without permission of the how's and why's of this famous barnyard animal.

Down in the NYC's Financial District, there has long stood a statue of a bull (as in "the bull market", I presume). It is near the Stock Exchange, and as such, stockbrokers pass by it every day. I read a while back that if you look closely, you will notice that the testicles on the statue are brilliantly burnished -- from the hands of myriad stockbrokers rubbing the statue there every day for luck on their way to work. [Kimberly Wadsworth, 01/14/2003]

[RA: The 3 1/2 ton bronze statue of a "Charging Bull" was sculptor Arturo Di Modica's artistic statement about the stock market's Black Monday in Oct 1987. Without permission, Di Modica placed the bull on Wall Street in 1989. It was moved a few blocks southwest to Bowling Green Park at the end of Broadway.]

After a short wait in line for our chance to pose for and snap a few pictures came. The only thing I rubbed were his horns. Yes, it is that famous, there was a line to take his picture. Next, our tour took us over to the World Trade Center location but there is not a whole lot to see there and soon it was back on the train heading north to Central Park. Before entering the park we walked past the Dakota Apartment Building, the scene of John Lennon's murder on December 8, 1980. Ironically, as I type this on July 7 I hear on the radio that today is Ringo Starr's sixty-ninth birthday. As a music lover I can only wonder the great amount of music Lennon would have written in the past 29 years had he lived. Upon entering Central Park is Strawberry Fields, a parcel of land dedicated to the memory of the former Beatle. Rest in peace John Lennon.

Shortly after, like most tourists, we found ourselves standing with our mouths open staring up at the Empire State Building. We declined the chance for a quick elevator ride to the top for between 20 and 40 bucks depending on what huckster you talked to on the sidewalk in front of the building. Having just completed a hike across Pennsylvania, New Jersey, and New York where mountain top vistas were enjoyed every day, free. After seeing everything of interest and eating as much food as our shrunken bellies could hold, it was back on the train heading north. It is amazing how fast two old guys traveling alone without luggage can see this great city. It was a great side trip as this part of town is impressively clean with very few urban campers, (bums) begging or threatening you for a handout. Sandy would definitely come here.

The return trip to Georgia went as planned and for two days, I enjoyed the luxuries of living in a more civilized surrounding. I quickly fell back into my normal lifestyle, taking essentials such as daily showers, microwave ovens, not pitching a tent on a rock and my nightly peanut butter and jelly sandwich for granted. On my third day off the trail the Giardia Gods unleashed on me a case of the most wicked diarrhea I have ever taken part in. I will spare the details but think Hurricane Katrina. I have seen my doctor and two others; I have e-mailed a Shaman in Alaska and participated in a colonoscopy and an upper endoscopy not to mention all the medicine in pill and powder form. As I finish this year's addition of my trail journal on August 7, 2009, I still carry the Giardia bug or more than likely the antibiotics taken to kill the Giardia also killed the good bacteria in my stomach. A person's stomach could be compared to a septic tank. If the bacteria in the tank dies the system stops working. Right now, I am drinking Dannon Activia Yogurt hoping it will restore my digestive system. The doctors all tell me this is not life threatening and I thank them for their time and advise but after more than two months the old bung hole is getting kind of tender.

CHAPTER FOUR

September 13, 2010

New York 22 to Wallingford, VT

Intense Hiking

It was an abbreviated hike, lasting only 13 hiking days but intense hiking it was, averaging over 17 miles per day. We drove 940 miles from Tom's home in Brimley, Michigan to last year's stopping point just inside the New York border. Only half hour after parking the truck at 11 A.M., the Forty-Niners were back on the trail under cloudy skies and warm temperatures. This is the first year I will hike with only one hiking pole and to save weight Tom has elected to forgo his water filtration pump for Aqua Mura tablets. He will save a pound of pack weight with this move. Our spirits were high as was the humidity and within the first mile droplets of sweat were dripping off the end of my nose. It would be only the beginning of much perspiration, sore muscles, blistered feet, and long days and short nights to come.

After seven quick adrenalin-pumping miles, the "Welcome to Connecticut" sign appeared triggering a quick photo shoot before pressing on. It was great to be back on the trail but it was apparent that most of the small streams and creeks were dry. Before long a local hiker informed us the area was without measurable rainfall for the past 21 days. It would pose problems for us throughout the first week of our hike. All hikers like to get water from a running spring, something coming right out of the hillside but on at least one occasion Tom treated what he referred to as frog water. He took pictures of two sad looking spring peepers looking up at him as he lowered the water level in their home.

We soon entered a hardwood forest made up mostly of oaks. The big hardy trees were in the process of shedding their acorns and supplying a prolific squirrel population with their winter's food. The acorns were so many they at times caused a dangerous situation as when stepped on they acted like marbles.

The first day out the trail was all ours other than two south bounders, one from Georgia and the other from Alabama, both with intentions of going all the way to Springer Mountain, Georgia. Camp that first night was at Schaghticoke Mountain Campsite. The day stretched into night, our tents were pitched with headlights as daylight said goodnight to us at about 7:30. Completing a 15-mile day, it was impossible at that time to know it would be one of our low mileage days. Such fun awaited us.

Morning came at 5 A.M. and hiking half hour later with no breakfast in our bellies due to the shortage of water. It was over an hour before we turned the headlights off and shortly after found water to replenish our bottles and cook oatmeal to satisfy an ever growling stomach.

The hike continued beneath the mammoth oak trees, bigger than what I am accustomed to seeing in the Upper Peninsula of Michigan as were the acorns very large. One eventually hit me in the back of my neck and rolled down inside my shirt. I thought I would leave it there but then my mind started playing games. What if it is something other than an acorn? Maybe a big black spider. My backpack has never been removed so quickly. With shirt pulled out of my pants an acorn fell to the ground. Life was good. Other than some beautiful scenery and two turkeys running across the trail it was the highlight of my day.

I shortly met three day hikers, a woman and two men all over 70 years of age. I did not tell them but it sure is good to see this. They give me inspiration.

An almost 18-mile day concluded at our destination, the Caesar Brook Campsite at around 5:30 that afternoon. My legs were tired, really tired but at least there would be company tonight. Red, a thru hiker from Iowa joined us about half an hour later. He came up with one of the more interesting reasons I have yet heard of to spend five or 6 months hiking the A.T. His theory is that most married men die before their wives do so he came to the conclusion that with him being gone for half a year his wife could kind of practice him being dead. Of course if anything major came up she could just call him. The guy deserves all the credit as it seems to be working. I did not find out what Red did for a living but I think he would have made a heck of a politician or used car salesmen.

I was in my tent and sleeping by 8 P.M., not turning once until six the next morning. The sleep would be needed as today would turn into a 20-mile day. My feet have already started causing problems. Every year I seem to develop blisters in one place or another despite the preventive duct tape applied on day one.

Later this afternoon would find us walking half a mile into Salisbury, Connecticut for restaurant food. Leaving town with a full belly and a little fresh fruit, heavy that it is I would eat it later that evening. Our intended campsite was only a mile from town but finding the advertised water supply like so many others, it had run dry. We dropped our packs along the trail, hiked back into town stopping at the first house, and knocked on the door. The middle-aged lady that answered could not have been more gracious. She was aware of the water shortage on the trail and told us to help ourselves to the outdoor water faucet. She is a fine lady and we appreciated her hospitality. After hiking back up to our packs with full water bottles and then another mile or so before setting up camp in a farmers hay field. Backing up just a bit to where we left our packs along the trail. In the five years spent on the trail I am not aware of even a single case of theft or anything mysteriously disappearing.

The next morning started at 6:30 A.M. with the first six miles up hill. The temperature was very cool, a local day hiker telling us that he had 38 degrees when he left home.

After four hours of walking the state of Connecticut's 51 miles were behind us. We entered Massachusetts knowing it too would go quickly as the trail runs only 90 miles before entering Vermont. We stopped and talked briefly with a small band of merry hikers from Cambridge, England. Young and looking very proper for folks calling Cambridge home, they more appeared to be touring a museum in Manhattan than hiking the A.T.

Thus far, Tom and I have been hiking together or Tom has been a good distance ahead. I am feeling sluggish and somewhat lethargic this year as opposed to the past three years. I already know what the problem is, my diet consists this year of more protein and less carbohydrates and my body cannot function well without the carbs. It would be hard to understand what my head was processing when I bought a hundred protein bars for this trip. The darn things are producing energy for my body like wet firewood produces heat.

A short hike today of 13 miles, knowing that heavy rain is forecast the chance to hold up at the Glen Brook Lean-to is welcomed. I enjoyed one of my favorite meals that day, instant mashed potatoes mixed with a foil packet of salmon topped with instant chicken gravy. No way I would eat this at home but on the trail it is just the best. Shortly after eating, Sasquatch walked into camp, a recent graduate of

Furman University. He had a rather unique way of staying dry in that he fashioned a rather large umbrella to fit into his pack belt. A young man but somewhat old school as he rolled his own cigarettes and with keeping only a paper journal, he carried none of the wireless gadgets most people his age could not do without.

Because of the coming rain, the night was spent in the lean-to. Built in the 1960's it provided space for six lending comfortable conditions for just the three of us. The next morning I mentioned that it was the first shelter on the entire trail that was not the home to countless mice. Tom in his infinite wisdom remarked, "Probably lot's of snakes around." Sometimes the truth is not comforting, I was quite happy to be leaving the Glen Brook Lean-to even thou last night's rain clouds were not yet empty. It turns out the rains are a contradiction. We curse it as it makes the rocks, roots and the trail in general slippery. Our very expensive rain gear promises to keep the rain out and for the most part it delivers on that end. It does not breathe and wick the perspiration away from our bodies as stated in the advertisements. On the other hand the rain is celebrated as it will replenish the streams, creeks and springs that hikers so depend on for our drinking water.

Our goal today is 20 miles away, Mt. Wilcox South Lean-to, leaving us 35 miles from our mail drop in Dalton, Massachusetts. The rain stops before noon but the sky remains overcast with high humidity eliminating any chance of damp gear becoming dry. Later this afternoon walking through a farmer's

131

cornfield we each liberated a cob, thinking it would be a culinary treat. It was not. Cold uncooked field corn is nowhere on the same page as cold uncooked sweet corn that I remember enjoying as a young boy. The next point of interest was Shays' Rebellion Monument located on South Egremont Road. Tom and I had a short discussion as to what this rebellion was all about. Both of us remembered it from high school but neither one could pinpoint exactly what its purpose was. I made a note in my journal to Google it when I returned home and so I have. Here is a very brief explanation:

Shays' Rebellion, 1786–87, armed insurrection by farmers in W Massachusetts against the state government. Debt-ridden farmers, struck by the economic depression that followed the American Revolution, petitioned the state senate to issue paper money and to halt foreclosure of mortgages on their property and their own imprisonment for debt as a result of high land taxes. Sentiment was particularly high against the commercial interests who controlled the state senate in Boston, and the lawyers who hastened the farmers' bankruptcy by their exorbitant fees for litigation. When the state senate failed to undertake reform, armed insurgents in the Berkshire Hills and the Connecticut valley, under the leadership of Daniel Shays and others, began (Aug., 1786) forcibly to prevent the county courts from sitting to make judgments for debt. In September they forced the state supreme court at Springfield to adjourn. Early in 1787, Gov. James Bowdoin appointed Gen. Benjamin Lincoln to command 4,400 men against the rebels. Before these troops arrived at Springfield, Gen. William Shepard's soldiers there had repelled an attack on the federal arsenal. The rebels, losing several men, had dispersed, and Lincoln's troops pursued them to Petersham, where they were finally routed. Shays escaped to Vermont. Most of the leaders were pardoned almost immediately, and Shays was finally pardoned in June, 1788. The rebellion influenced Massachusetts's ratification of the U.S. Constitution; it also swept Bowdoin out of office and achieved some of its legislative goals.

That will be the history lesson for the day. I can only imagine what Mr. Shay would have to say about our current state of affairs in Washington.

At this point, almost 70 miles into our hike, potable water remains our biggest problem. The trail now runs along a most beautiful river, the Housatonic, a wide, shallow rambling body of water polluted with PCB's. More interesting reading from Google:

From about 1932 until 1977 the river received PCB pollution discharges from the General Electric plant at Pittsfield, MA.[2] Although the water quality has improved in recent decades, the river continues to be contaminated by PCBs.

Our next stop was at a small coffee shop off U.S. 7 looking for tap water but were told the ground water was so polluted with fertilizer runoff it was unsafe to drink. The woman running the shop sold us a gallon of bottled water for about two bucks. We most certainly would have paid more. Later in the day, still following the Housatonic signs posted at the river bank warning against drinking or eating fish or frogs from the river. We were still dwarfed by huge oak trees with an abundance of acorns but noticed very few squirrels. Perhaps they drink the water. Sad, it looked like a great place for not only fishing but for kids to cool off on a hot summer day. The state of this river and the ground water situation surprised both of us; after all, this is Massachusetts. We continued on, noting that the poplar trees are shedding their leaves while the oaks and maples were just starting with the first hint of their seasonal spectacular. I do not know one wild flower from another but they are as plentiful as they are beautiful. Our 20 miles today ended at the Mt. Wilcox South Lean-to in mid-afternoon. A small but ample spring right on the trail just before arriving resolved our water problems. At least for today and it is always nice to have water close to the campsites.

Next morning saw us up and moving by 5:30 A.M. Not bad considering I had some minor troubles with my stove before making coffee and oatmeal. This year I foolishly cut my oatmeal ration from two bags to one. The rational being I would not miss the extra calories and of course shaving a little weight is always at the forefront of my thinking. Next year will see a return to my double bag ration. Today the hike will be 17 miles and the night will be spent at a motel just a tenth mile off the trail. It has been six days without a shower, the weather has been hot and cold, wet and dry and there is an odor about us. Our legs move today with adrenalin pumping and only happy thoughts enter our minds. Hot showers, warm dry beds, and restaurant food delivered to our door. For some reason the miles came easy. The trail took us through a pasture with several head of beef cattle; it seemed the beasts were well used to hikers, almost begging to have their pictures taken. The trail also passed numerous apple trees but to our dismay none of them were worthy of a treat. Check-in time at the motel came about three that afternoon. It seems to be true that as the trail winds north the more it costs for a night out of the weather. After showers, washing clothes, eating salads and pizza and sitting on a soft clean bed while I write this in my journal the money is negligible.

After machine made coffee the next morning with a little left over pizza for breakfast it was back to the trail. Nineteen miles from Dalton, Massachusetts, our first and only mail drop for this year. According to our guidebooks today would be our chance to meet the Cookie Lady, Marilyn Wiley who lives just a tenth of a mile off the trail. Marilyn and Roy Wiley own and operate a blueberry farm and is a must stop for hikers. As Tom and I walked into the yard a barking dog met us followed by Marilyn with a basket of cookies for which she is famous. A water spigot is provided for hikers and free camping is available with permission first. When in season you can pick your own blueberries at reasonable rates. In addition, we enjoyed hard-boiled eggs, half dozen for a buck fifty, what a treat.

It was mid-afternoon when we rolled into Dalton. As per the guidebook   the home of Tom Levardi was an easy find, a longtime friend of hikers on the A.T. Tom provided tent space in his back yard, shuttle service, and a fleet of bicycles for use around town. Tom and I were the only hikers in town that night and with threatening rain Tom graciously allowed us to bed down on his front porch. Being located right in town with houses close by I had to wonder what his neighbors think in the height of hiking season when he might have 20 tents set up in the backyard. My answer came shortly after as the lady next-door came over with cake and ice cream for the three of us. She has to be one very understanding person.

As happy as it made us to have a roof over our heads that night sleep was hard to find due to the heavy traffic on the street just 20 feet from our porch/campsite. After five hours of much tossing and turning and little sleep it is off to North Adams, 23 miles away where we would rent a car and spend a day driving back to New York for Tom's truck. After driving both vehicles north to our stopping point where Toms truck would be left. With this accomplished it was back to the post office in Dalton for our drop boxes. Tom has this all figured out days in advance. I offer moral support.

Along the way I had to stop at a Verizon store so I could replace my phone that no longer worked. After taking my information the friendly salesperson informed me I was eligible for a free update. Free! That made me feel good about my decision to contract with Verizon in the first place. By the time I walked out the door with my free upgrade I was 50 dollars poorer. He must have seen me coming. Continuing on to Dalton for our much needed re-supply boxes there are noticeable few and sometimes no fast food restaurants in the villages and towns in this area. Although it seems they are blessed with many of what appear to be Mom & Pop stores. The country side is awesomely beautifully to the point of making a guy want to quit his real job and move here to raise sheep and grow organic tomatoes. Yes, it is that lovely and the number of pumpkins growing on the hillsides are more than I have ever seen. Perhaps they send them all to Wal-Mart in the city.

Once back in Dalton I get a big surprise as my drop box is nowhere to be found. The post office is small and the lady behind the counter looked frantically for the parcel but to no avail. Disappointedly it was off to the grocery store. Missing the dehydrated food along with the maps for the rest of this year's hike put me in a less than happy mood. Next year I will either pay the extra money for insurance or go with FedEx. As I type this out on November 4 I still have not received the box at my return address.

After returning to North Adams and dropping the rental off the plan is to hike seven miles to the Seth Warner Shelter. We walked out of Massachusetts and into Vermont, another state down, three to go but they will not come easily as the saying I have heard many times from experienced hikers, "You may have most of the miles done but most of the work remains." I am looking forward to the Green Mountains of Vermont, the White Mountains of New Hampshire and the pure ruggedness of Maine but it will test my ability as well as my mental fortitude.

As the trail crosses into Vermont the A.T. joins the Long Trail for about 105 miles to the "Maine Junction" at Willard Gap. From there the Long Trail continues north to Canada, 168 miles and the A.T. in a more northeast direction to Katahdin. Our arrival at the shelter came an hour after entering Vermont. When done eating I sat in the shelter with my note-pad trying to re-cap our journey this far. I am again using a small recording device to dictate any thoughts running through my head during the day while walking as my memory fails me time and again. Even with my recorder some things get discombobulated, I forget the order of things, even the day of the week. It is at this shelter another hiker told the story of a novice that was bitten by the allure of this footpath. Having read a few books on the A. T. this particular guy broke the news to his wife of his desire to thru-hike the trail. Knowing her husband well her support of such a venture was less than enthusiastic. She warned him that if he was going to spend in excess of $1,500 on gear for such a trip he had better plan on doing at least half the trail to get his money's worth. As the story unfolds the guy hiked for ten days, barely getting out of Georgia when he realized his wife was right but also remembering her words when he left home. He hated hiking and trail life in general. He has been residing at a Motel 6 somewhere in Tennessee for the past three weeks.

The likelihood of us averaging 18 miles a day and reaching the truck Sunday night is within our grasp. We camped out at Melville Nauheim Shelter our first night back on the trail with two twenty something guys. One a recent college graduate with some kind of degree in writing. He was now employed at a nearby organic farm and told us the demand for such products was booming. The other guy was still in school and talked the people that make such decisions into allowing him to hike the entire Long Trail for a paper he needed to complete before graduation. Good kids both of them, completely relaxed and entertaining around their 61-year-old campmates. The company is more than welcome as this year we more or less have the trail and the shelters to ourselves as the thru-hiker class of 2010 is well ahead of us on their way to the summit of Katahdin.

Our legs are well rested from yesterday's short hike and being back on the trail at 5:30 A.M. feels great. An hour later the big ball of fire in the east treats us to a most amazing sunrise. From a sailors prospective it would have been a warning of impending bad weather but as hikers it was just one of the many sights this trail treats us to on a daily bases. Now as the conclusion of this year's hike is at hand, high mileage rather than great vistas seems to be the target. I think it is like that all the time with us. This trail offers up a challenge to Tom and myself and it is a challenge we seem to welcome. Obsession with high mileage is nothing new to some long distance hikers, for one reason or another some of us will hike until weary and beyond but still find the energy to do another mile or so. The saying on the trail is, "Hike your own hike." Most injuries are a direct result of such thinking but it is the game we play. Doing such a short hike this year our bodies did not have a chance to become trail hardened and from day one I have felt stiff and sore in every part of my being, nothing serious but the nagging pain will not leave my body, only fooling me by moving from one place to another.

We found room in the shelter for another night, sharing it with only one other guy. His water bottle was wrapped in a Bush-Cheney bumper sticker. I inquired if it aroused any controversy along the trail and he replied in the negative. That same evening four hikers from Georgia came in and pitched tents off to the side of the shelter. All four appeared to be in their fifties and have been coming to the trail as a team for the past 14 years, covering as much ground as time permits.

Again this year as the trail takes us through trailheads a little time is taken to read bumper stickers. It seems to me that I have more interest in checking out a parking lot than I do a particular vista that is highlighted in the guidebook. One huge difference in the political stickers up here in the northeast is that most favor the Democrat Party as opposed to down south where the Republicans carry the day. In addition, foreign automobiles are in the vast majority in these parts. I took a count at two trailheads, the first had eight imports and only one American brand and in another the score was seven to one, again in favor of the Hondas and Toyotas.

I noticed today several flocks of geese heading to someplace where the ponds do not freeze and the food is more plentiful. The temperature reached almost

80 today. I wonder if this makes them second-guess their decision to head south or do they know that their long journey requires such an early start. So they do a thru-hike twice a year. Does that qualify as a yo-yo?

Friday morning bright and early and hiking at 5 A.M. Soon a big red ball of misery will rise in the east. It makes us carry more water and before long our shirts will no longer be dry. It is going to be a very warm day, close to 85 degrees. As the day progresses the hills come one after another, I notice the rocks are sweating as am I, like a rented mule. By noon the cool mountain spring water I filtered this morning is warm mountain spring water but I continue to drink, it gets the job done. One of the few hikers we meet today is "Steps," besides his love of hiking he also runs a hostel for cross-country bike riders when he is back home in Michigan.

The area we are now walking is heavily used during the prime hiking season so for this reason a small fee is charged for use of the shelters or tenting areas. Caretakers are present throughout the hiking season for trail maintenance, hiker information, and to collect the fees. One such caretaker, a young lady we came across at Stratton Pond was one unfriendly person. Tom and I, hiking together, greeted her with a "hello" and received no acknowledgement what-so-ever. Shortly after Tom agreed to fill out a survey for a Forest Service worker sitting on a log at shores edge. While filling out the questionnaire the same caretaker dragged a canoe down to the water and walked past us again not uttering a single word. With a full backpack on she pushed off from shore without the benefit of a life jacket. The Forest Service guy informed us that this was his second encounter with the girl and he has received the same treatment. I do not know if she was having a bad day or whatever but if she intends to continue working with the public she definitely needs an attitude adjustment. We filled our water bottles and continued on, somewhat perplexed I guess. Our targeted shelter was reached in the late afternoon but to our dismay the spring was dry. Again, forced by the lack of water to change plans. The next chance to sleep with a roof over our heads was Bromley Shelter, five miles north. Back on the trail munching on red and white colored candy's that Tom carries for just this sort of situation. The darn things are the size of a mothball and must be made of pure sugar as it takes only three minutes to dissolve plus you can almost hear your teeth rotting away. But they work, it's not the first time those little round balls of sugar carried us a few extra miles in the late afternoon. We settled in and slept well after a 23-mile day, having no inkling that tomorrows hike would be even longer.

The plan was to hike to Little Rock Pond Shelter and it was easily accomplished but the shelter was no more, it was gone, history. More proof that for next year I will have to acquire an up to date guidebook. The possibility of tenting in the area was good but the truck sat just six miles away. Already tired from yesterdays march, the thought of a shower and a mattress to sleep on was a bit to overcome so back to the trail it was. It meant 48 miles in the last two days and dark fell before reaching the parking lot but within minutes it was full speed ahead in a southwest direction at 65 miles per hour rather than two miles per hour in a northeast direction.

Another year on the trail completed, short that it was the tally came in at 229 miles for a little over 16 miles a day. This leaves us with 511 miles for next year, I have read and been told about the tough hiking ahead. The talk on the long ride home turned to ways of cutting pack weight. Our thoughts can now focus on about 70 miles in Vermont then New Hampshire's White Mountains and 282 miles to Katahdin in Maine.

CHAPTER FIVE

AUGUST 17, 2011

Wallingford, VT to Mt. Katahdin, ME

Big Mountains, Tough Hiking

Over four years have passed since my Grandson Justin and I took our first steps on the Appalachian Trail into a cool drizzle on Springer Mountain. At this point, after hiking 1,667 miles into 12 states have left me with a little over 500 miles from the northern terminus, Mt. Katahdin, Maine. Other hikers I have talked to and books I have read tell me that even though three quarters of the trail is behind me three quarters of the work remains.

"Ha, how can this be?" I repeatedly ask myself. I am not a rookie anymore. I know the ways of long distance hiking. I can do 20 mile days consecutively and if need be I can do 35 or more in a day, carrying a 32 pound pack on my back. I am convinced these words are spoken and written by uninformed writers and rookie hikers looking for an excuse not to hike in the White Mountains of New Hampshire or the rugged state of Maine where they don't build bridges over every water crossing but expect you to ford these streams and rivers in rushing water so darn cold your feet are numb well before reaching the opposite shore.

It was a long but uneventful trip from the central Upper Peninsula of Michigan to the trailhead in Wallingford, Vt. where last year's hike ended. We ate a quick breakfast at Mom's Restaurant in the small village of Wallingford. The food was superb and I knew it would be my last meal that did not go through the dehydration process for five days. Upon leaving the restaurant, I noticed my first "Obama 2012" bumper sticker. Interestingly I noticed only one other in the forty days spent in New England. Again this year Tom and I prowled parking lots reading words of wisdom on the backs of cars and noting American brands to foreign makes. The final tally was shocking; eight of 10 autos were manufactured in Japan or Europe. After parking the truck, checking, and re-checking our gear, Tom still forgot his camera. We set out full of enthusiasm walking south approximately 500 yards so this year's hike would begin at last year's exact stopping place. The Forty-Niners were reunited with the trail; it was an easy 13-mile hike that first day before stopping at the Governor Clement Shelter. With only a few other hikers around we opted to sleep in the three-sided stone shelter and it did get cold. Cold enough to have on all my clothes and still needing to use my tent as a cover.

I believe I spent all thirteen of those first miles

riding my mountain bike, at least in my head I thought of very little else. This is our fifth year of hiking but also my fifth year of riding and racing mountain bikes and after a good performance in my first two races I had to deal with missing the rest of the season. Not that there was ever a chance of not coming back to the trail but my wife even told me she could see me entering a new chapter in my retired life. I guess it was not hard to figure, bike magazines replaced hiking books, I spent more time riding and my garage took on the look of a bike shop. I rode that bike all the way to Hanover, New Hampshire but shortly after Mt. Moosilauke appeared and I believe I made peace with the trail and from that point on my head belonged to the Appalachian Trail.

After six miles the first day we crossed the Mill River via a suspension bridge dedicated to the memory of Robert Brugmann, who drowned several years ago while attempting to cross the swollen river. Also on day one six very friendly cows met us, they seemed to embrace any hiker that might have a bit of salt on their arms. Great vistas all around but the pictures taken that day were of the big friendly beasts. Hiking this time of year allowed us to eat sweet blackberries along the trail and sample apples that were much too tart to enjoy. The "500 miles to go" mark came and with it trail magic in the form of a cooler full of ice cold Mountain Due and a white plastic lawn chair to sit and relax for a minute. To the people that haul this stuff out in the woods, I can only say thank you through forums like this, as I or most other hikers will more than likely never meet you face to face. Even on the first day of a

40-day hike your kindness is appreciated and will never be forgotten.

In an attempt to save 20 ounces of pack weight I left my sleeping bag in the truck, carrying only a bag liner, space blanket, and a few "Orteil Toe Warmers" to keep warm at night. I was able to do this as we plan to rent a car in Hanover, come back to the truck and move it further north where it will be used as a re-supply source.

First thing the next morning, after oatmeal and coffee of course, we climbed 2,000 feet to Cooper Lodge, one of the few enclosed shelters on the trail. I took time there, as I would for the remainder of the trip to change socks and dry my shoes in the morning sunlight. This year I have made it a point to take better care of my feet. I found a product on-line called "benzoin compound" that when brushed on toughened the skin to a point of preventing blisters. It was messy to use, as even when dry it remained sticky making my feet look horribly dirty but it did reduce blistering on the soles and heels.

Even though I continue to ride my bike, signs begin to appear telling us the distance from Katahdin, which momentarily takes me off the bike and puts me on the trail.

Our campsite the second night was at Gifford Woods State Park. The cost was five bucks for a tent site, fifty cents for a five-minute hot shower but no soap and all the ice cream we cared to purchase at the park office. All things considered not a bad deal. Sleeping in my tent provided me with another 10 degrees of warmth so I slept much better tonight than last.

I was the first one out the next morning so of course the unpleasant chore of breaking the spider webs spun across the trail fell on my shoulders. Do they spend all night spinning those darn things, right at eye level? At times, I walked with my hiking pole held vertically out in front but for the most part, I took them on the chin, in my mouth or in my eyes. Disgusting, my only hope was to meet a south bounder and that did happen but not soon enough. He was also pleased to see me. We would continue to meet south bounders in the early part of our journey but they grew fewer and fewer as the days grew shorter. All north bounders need to finish this hike near the end of September or early October as the trails above tree line in Baxter State Park, home to Katahdin are eventual closed for the winter. The south bounders need to be out of New England and well on their way south at the same time.

Tom joined me as I stopped to pick small sweet blueberries along the trail. I asked him what type of food he might be eating had he remained back home and in his normal routine. I told him this being Friday it would be a fish fry for me unless I was racing the next morning then I would opt for a big plate of carbohydrate rich pasta. Tom, as he told me many times in the past four years thought eating Oreo cookies with a tall glass of cold milk would be as good as it gets. It is a fact that the only disagreement the two of us had in the 2,000 plus miles we hiked together was about Oreo cookies. I remember it was the third year out in a grocery store re-supplying when Tom asked if I cared to split a bag of Oreo's.

"Sure" I replied, "let's get double frosting." Tom was already reaching for the single frosting cookies. I am a sugar freak, "the more the better," has been my lifelong mantra. A brief discussion was followed by us both buying a bag of cookies; mine of course had the double frosting. It still gets a chuckle when it comes up today.

Last night we tented at Wintturi Shelter and again the temperature dropped into the 40's forcing me to break out my space blanket, sometimes called a Mylar blanket. It did a great job of keeping me warm but it also holds in a good deal of condensation giving me a rather humid feeling the next morning.

After a four-mile hike Saturday morning we walked two tenths of a mile on Vermont 12 to a farm stand called, "On the Edge." I don't know if they mean on the edge of the trail or on the edge of something else but they served ice cream, cold drinks, pies, cheese, smoked meat, and seasonal veggies and have picnic tables for us weary, smelly hikers to sit and relax. I cannot speak for all hikers but this is the sort of thing I just loved about the tail. This was the second occasion in three days of hiking that presented the opportunity to enjoy ice cream. So far this year the Forty-Niners are definitely smelling the roses and today the roses taste like strawberry ice cream and a locally made cheese. What a combination that was. Several other hikers were already there, one of them being a guy from Virginia with the trail name of Rain Gear. As often happens on the trail we hiked with him another day or so into Hanover but then lost track of him for several weeks. Later that day on Cloudland Road it was another stop for still more ice cream. The time of wine and roses would soon end and the mountains would begin. Bring them on; right now we are fat and sassy.

So far this year cell phone coverage has been average, close to towns and at higher elevation there was a good chance of making a call. What has changed dramatically from four years ago is the acceptance of them. Many hikers carried smart phones with the ability to send e-mail and surf the web but most importantly receive up to the minute local weather reports. My dumb phone did no such thing but I quickly made friends with anyone toting a smart one. Another difference I see between this year and 2007 is the use of performance enhancing supplements. The gel packs made by Power Bar and others seemed to lead the way. I have used them for bike races the past five years but this is the first time on the trail. I believe they do work but in a limited way, there is no magic to hike that last three miles of the day, its one heavy step at a time.

Again today I walked past a sign telling me of my distance from Katahdin. The miles are winding down but winding slowly and there is a ton of walking to do before reaching the Big Mountain in Maine. I would bet that most non-hikers have even heard of Mt. Katahdin. From my perspective this mountain is so meaningful to hiker's worldwide that when you arrive at Katahdin you have reached the icon of the hiking world. When I first saw it while standing on Abol Bridge on the second to last day of this hike, my first thought was of Mt. Rainier. Katahdin stands only a little over 5,200 feet while Rainier is over 14,000 feet so I guess the comparison was only in my head but the beauty of Katahdin certainly matches that of any in the lower United States.

On Sunday, I saw my first deer and found blackberries so abundant and sweet I spent 45 minutes in one patch alone. We also walked into West Hartford to the "Full Belly Deli," for a second breakfast of blueberry pancakes with ham and real Vermont Maple Syrup. On the trail the plastic hoses hooked to the maple trees for collecting sap is ever present.

The last night before entering Hanover was spent at the Thistle Hill Shelter. Some of the hikers we are seeing every day and I even remember some of their names. There is Mouse, Toad, 9 Lives, Jedi, and Blue Foot. The first four in their early twenties and mostly college graduates and mostly without jobs. Blue Foot, mid 40s I would guess works for Whole Foods, a high-end grocery retailer known to most that have shopped in one of their stores as "Whole Paycheck." It puts shopping for food at another level, visiting one of their stores is a great adventure in gathering the food we eat. Blue Foot was on a six-month sabbatical from Whole Foods to thru hike the A. T. John Mackey, the cofounder and CEO of the company has also hiked the entire trail.

Jedi is a soft-spoken very polite young man from Alabama with an English degree but surprisingly no accent.

151

At 1:30 this afternoon we crossed the Connecticut River into our 13th state, New Hampshire and shortly after into Hanover, home to Dartmouth College. I was not sure what to expect from this New England town with an Ivy League School and no McDonalds. Most towns along the trail have two McDonalds and no colleges. Any fears I carried were unfounded as the town's people were great. The restaurant owners gave us free pizza, bagels and pastry. The people at the library welcomed us as Tom spent time on a computer and I read a week's worth of newspapers. There was time to kill, as the car rental place did not open until Monday. The car was needed to move the truck further north where again it would be used as a re-supply point. For supper it was the food co-op rather than a restaurant where I put together a Caesar salad, fresh made bagels and a bottle of chocolate goat's milk and then ice cream for dessert. It appeared to be the only grocery store in town and was comparable to a Whole Foods store, very good but a little hard on a hikers wallet. Once our appetites were satisfied it was off to an area behind the Dartmouth soccer fields where several of us pitched our tents. A light rain fell as I zipped my tent closed for the night and what a long wet night it would be. This is the fourth year on my Eureka Spitfire Ultralite tent so I should have been smart enough to reseal the seams or at least check them but of course, I did not. I slept very little between mopping up water and bitching at myself for being so careless. The next day after a very good breakfast at Lou's and then a five dollar shower at the

Recreation Center I set out for the Mountain Goat Outfitter to purchase seam sealer while Tom stayed behind to wash clothes. As you hikers all know if Tom was washing our clothes, I was walking through town in my rain gear and nothing but my rain gear on a bright sunny morning. In a non-hiker town, I would have drawn suspicion as some sort of vagrant but here in Hanover, N. H. I turned not one head. As I ambled the streets of this college town I meet well-dressed fast walking men, most carrying briefcases. Occasionally I would catch their eye and wonder if they are the men leading lives of quiet desperation as Thoreau wrote about. Were they secretly wishing it were they walking the streets of some far off hiker town in rain gear and Crocks or were they thanking their lucky stars that they were on their way to work rather than the A.T. The town is well laid out for a person on foot, as everything needed was within walking distance and there is a free city bus service connecting Hanover with several other nearby towns. We used this service to pick up the rental car. On the bus, I overheard people talking about going to Wal-Mart but I have no idea where it might be.

On the way to the bus stop another hiker called Wild Bill stopped to chat. He really looked like a Wild Bill and was hiking with a dog that was the better looking of the two. He, the dog also smelled better. Anyway, Bill was doing a yo-yo. Having spent the last six months walking from Georgia to Maine he was now walking from Maine to Georgia. He must have a short memory. He also told us that five bucks was too much for a shower so he would forgo that little chore, I

153

wished him well.

After picking up the rental car the drive back to Wallingford, Vt. went quickly. I then followed Tom in the truck about 100 trail miles to Crawford Notch. As we drove north, the White Mountains were upon us, they were striking but knowing I would soon be walking through them, they were also daunting. This was a well-planned strategy by Tom worked out weeks before but little did he or anyone else know Hurricane Irene would change the campaign for thousands of hikers.

We also had mail drops waiting in Glencliff, N.H., only 40 trail miles from Hanover, thus allowing us to hike with lighter packs. From here, boxes were also mailed to Andover, Maine. There is more to this hiking than just walking down the trail and there is no one better at planning than Tom. As I have said before this is a good thing for me as I am as unorganized as they come.

With the truck moved, we spent the night at a Motel 8 in White River Junction. It was good to take a shower on consecutive days, lie on a soft bed, and watch T. V. As Tom pumped gas in the rental the next morning, I noticed construction workers stopping in for coffee and maybe a sandwich. What I really noticed were the long sleeved flannel shirts they wore. The same type I would have on back home when I knew the day was going to stay cool. Autumn, while not immediately on us was giving fair warning it soon will be.

At 9:30 A.M. Tuesday morning the march out of

Hanover began. The trail out of town carries us gently up hill and is laden with pine needles making it easy on the soles of my feet and maybe good for my soul but of course it would not continue. There are serious mountains ahead of us.

Eleven miles out of Hanover I reached the 2,290-foot summit of Moose Mountain. Normally a mountain this size would be hiked up and down without special consideration but in October of 1968 a Northeast Airplane with 42 persons on board crashed and burned here killing all but ten passengers. Part of the wreckage remains on the mountain.

With well rested legs and light packs, the 17-mile hike to Trapper John Shelter was relatively easy. Spice Dude, an acquaintance from last year also camped there. He started the trail in 2000 and hoped to finish this year.

Another character we met along the trail was Frenchie and his dog Miki. Frenchie was a citizen of Quebec and recently returned from France where he earned a masters degree in sustained tourism.

The next night was spent at the Hikers Welcome Hostel on N.H. 25. The going price was about 25 bucks for a bunk, outside shower, and use of an outside washer and dryer. It is always nice to spend a night off the trail and some hostels are fresh and sparkling but this was not one of them. I am not complaining, I was glad to be there and after all, it is a hiker hostel. I ate microwave pizza and drank an endless supply of off brand cola products that were reasonably priced. I found an old Lance Armstrong book upstairs and killed a few hours reading it. Hurricane Irene was making her way up the east coast with a fury and with the long-range potential of interrupting our hike. The weatherman reported 40-foot waves off New York City; it is not encouraging to the 10 hikers gathered around the T. V. in the common area of the hostel. As I said earlier, in the immortal words of Alfred E. Neuman, "What me worry." I was reading a book; Tom was reading the hiker guide and working out a contingency plan in the event Irene would force us off the trail.

It was a place to meet old friends, as Miss Janet of Erwin, Tennessee was there running shuttles. She closed her hostel a couple years ago. Tom also met Bag of Tricks, an acquaintance from several years back and Spice Dude also spent the night. Spice Dude is an interesting guy; he loved politics and would turn any talk into a political discussion. Both of us being of the Libertarian persuasion I agreed with most of what he had to say. He loved Calvin Coolidge. How many friends do you have that love Calvin Coolidge?

The Hostel is located right across the street from the Post Office where most hikers send drop boxes containing heavier clothing to contend with the colder temperatures that would soon be experienced in the White Mountains.

Friday, August 26th Tom and I walked out of the Hikers Welcome Hostel at 6:30 A.M. Our backpacks were loaded, giving you some idea of the difficult hike that awaits us, five days food for only 53 miles of trail, and extra warm clothing for today will be our first in the big boy mountains. Moosilauke will be the first of many coming our way, a climb of 3,800 feet spread over six miles to the summit. We made good time but the promised vistas were not to be, a light, cold rain fell w th the fog cutting visibility to 15 feet. It was not discouraging as the guidebook informed us of countless above tree line vistas yet to come. This was the White Mountains, the real work has started but the Lady Irene, the hurricane holds all the cards.

Eliza Brook Shelter provided our shelter for the tenth night but the word on the trail was to evacuate, high winds and heavy rain would force the Forest Service to close the trails and huts.

The Appalachian Mountain Club maintains approximately 122 miles of trails and an extensive collection of enclosed lodges spaced a short day's hike apart that sleep 36 to 90 people. The cost per night being around $100. Fortunately, shelters and tent sites are also available. They also run a shuttle system that goes from one trailhead to the next.

It was about a six mile hike the next day to the Lonesome Lake Hut and from there a two-mile side trail leading to a bus stop. From there the shuttle carried us to Crawford Notch where Tom's truck was parked. Having a vehicle at our disposal gave us many options not afforded to those hikers that would depend on their thumb to hitch a ride. A motel in Twin Mountain would be our home for tonight. Sunday came with heavy rain but only light wind. Tom packed and re-packed his backpack; I napped and watched T. V. The coverage of Hurricane Irene was a little over the top, going non-stop without even a short update on other world events. Afterward I read the media was heavily criticized for this and rightly so. The storm left us that afternoon with Monday bringing sunny skies with a seven-day forecast of great hiking weather. Tom, myself, and a few other hikers went back on the trail despite the fact it was still officially closed.

Two days later, we would meet Rob and Keith, friends of Tom from Michigan. The plan was for them to hike through the Presidential Range with us. Another factor in our favor was having two vehicles to again position Tom's truck where it could be used as a re-supply point. This may sound trivial but saving a few pounds in the food bag always lifts a hiker's spirits. This is perhaps the most scenic section of the whole trail but the vistas do not come cheap as we pay full retail, the cost to our bodies is tremendous. Other authors much more proficient than I have already used all the big descriptive words to illustrate these mountains so I will only add that if you have a chance do not pass up an opportunity to visit this area.

Tom, myself, and one other hiker got our butts chewed out for cooking in the shelter at Ethan Pond. It is a good policy to not cook in the shelters if for no other reason it leaves the mice little chance of finding food. And more importantly bears. It is also a policy that few follow simply because it is more comfortable to sit in a shelter and cook than it is on a rock or log. Because of heavy usage of the shelters in the White Mountains, the AMC employs what are known as "ridge runners." These people actually live on site and are responsible for keeping the shelter and privy in an orderly way. They also collect a fee, eight bucks if you spend the night. At our remaining camp sites, we made it a point to ask the ridge runner about restrictions on cooking. Every one told us to cook anywhere we wanted.

The initial plan was to spend the night there but our state of mind was a little uncomfortable being around this particular ridge runner. The truck was only three miles away at Crawford Notch so the decision was made to hike out. It turned out well as within 30 minutes Rob and Keith met us hiking in. The four of us returned to the truck and spent another night at the motel in Twin Mountain.

The hike with Rob and Keith two days after the storm went well enough despite a good deal of water on the trail. Because of a road washout on U.S. 302, all hikers were forced to park four miles from the trailhead at Crawford Notch. It was a short hiking day, only picking up seven trail miles before stopping at Nauman Tent site for the night. The landscape in this area is exceptionally rocky and uneven thus the wooden tent platforms provided by the trail maintainers. I do not have a stand-alone tent, it must be staked out and this presented a problem setting up on a wood deck but eventually with enough rope, I made it work. Before pitching our tents, Tom noticed one corner of the platform was much lower than the rest so he shimmed it up with rocks. Rob, an engineer, has a level on his smart phone. Makes one wonder what else those things will do.

The better part of the next day took us up majestic Mt. Washington but unfortunately visibility on top the 6,288 footer was absolute zero. This mountain is also accessible by automobile and a cog railroad. I read in my guidebook that in 2007 eight hikers were arrested for mooning said cog railroad. Media around the world ran the story. Must have been a slow news day. The summit building is operated by the New Hampshire Division of Parks and Recreation where they maintain a snack bar and other stuff I had little interest in. I consumed three large pieces of pizza, two diet Cokes, and a few candy bars all in about 20 minutes. Keith was feeling poorly and opted to ride the train down while Rob, Tom, and I hiked down to the Osgood Tent site and spent the night there.

A short five-mile stroll the next morning and we were back at Pinkham Notch where Keith was waiting. From here, he and Rob headed to the coast of Maine for fresh seafood and then back to Michigan. Tom and I in the truck went to the White Mountain Hostel on U.S. 2 in Gorham for the night. This is one of the top three hostels I have stayed at to this point. Exceptionally clean and the price of admission includes breakfast. Next morning we drove back to Pinkham where the truck will stay until wives Sandy and Lynn pick it up on their way to Millinocket at the conclusion of the hike. Again, on the trail with light food bags as in two days the trail would return us to the White Mountain Hostel where the majority of our food was left.

The next day it took us eleven hours to cover only 13 miles. The climbing up is tough but some of the down hills are harder. At times, the only way is to slide down on the seat of your pants while holding onto branches of spruce trees one after another until reaching the bottom. And praying the spruce trees hold.

As we hiked across the Presidential Range, I knew exactly what mountain I was on and what mountain lay ahead but once done with them the mountains of less prominence seem to be only obstacles in my quest of Katahdin. I find myself longing for the trails of Virginia, good old dirt and grass rather than the rock and tree roots I have been exposed to for most of this year's hike. I feel like I am chasing the white blazes only to achieve the end. I liken the trail to that of a prizefighter with a fast and powerful jab, constantly hitting my body, every jab taking something away from my resolve but never landing a knockout punch. Excluding a serious injury I will not quit, I will climb the big mountain in Maine. I talked to another older hiker today, it sounded like he was having a bad day. The guy told me upon returning home his hiking gear was going to be sold on E-bay and he was buying a bowling ball. He went on to tell me the ball would only weigh 16 pounds and while bowling you could drink beer and eat potato chips between frames. I wished him well and thought him to be a wise man.

It was late morning upon returning to the White Mountain Hostel where the rest of the day was spent checking gear and visiting with other hikers. I weighed myself here and came in at 180 pounds, down 10 in the first twenty days of hiking. I knew this could not continue so I rode into town with the hostel owner and purchased about 30 dollars worth of candy bars. The darn things felt like they weighed a ton but It was imperative that I stop losing weight. From here on the truck would not be available for use as a re-supply point but there would be the mail drop in Andover, Maine, only three days away.

At breakfast the next morning at the White Mountain Hostel six hungry hikers gathered around the table. The group included Doug, a child psychiatrist, Little Tractor 88, a stockbroker, a young girl that I do not remember her name was working on her PhD, a young man to my left had some sort of degree in biology, Tom has a degree from Michigan State so with the exception of me, I was having breakfast with a rather talented group. This reminded me of the famous J.F.K. quote.

President John F. Kennedy welcomed 49 Nobel Prize winners to the White House in 1962, saying, "I think this is the most extraordinary collection of talent, of human knowledge, that has ever been gathered at the White House, with the possible exception of when Thomas Jefferson dined alone."

This certainly was not the White House but the White Mountain Hostel. I doubt Jefferson ever dined here but for some reason it popped into my head. Long distance hiking does crazy things to a guy's head. Remember that deal about running Boston? I first heard the term "hiker midnight" at this hostel. It is simply whatever time it gets dark and every day we were losing minutes of valuable daylight hiking time thus hiker midnight came earlier every day.

After breakfast Tom and I were the first back on the trail. A light cool drizzle would be our companion. It turned into a 17-mile day, mostly in the rain. This effort put us at the Carlo Col Shelter but more importantly, our spirits were lifted as the last state came into play. This definitely called for a photo shoot at a sign that read, "Welcome to Maine, The Way Life Should Be." This brought a good chuckle as we were wet and the hiking was hard. This is not the first time I have been in this state. I spent approximately a year at the now defunct Loring Air Force Base way up north by Limestone. The next day would be no easier as the Mahoosuc Notch awaits us. This one-mile stretch is said to be the toughest on the entire trail. Rather than a hike, it is a scramble over, under, around, and between huge rocks. There would be no soft landing in the event of a fall. Two and a half hours of our hiking day was burned with this unbelievable challenging but fun section of trail. Both of us did a little bloodletting hiking the Notch but it is unlikely anyone gets through this thing unscathed.

Things got no easier the next day. The weather remained unstable, seeming to not know what it wanted to do. According to our maps and guidebook, the trail would remain a formidable foe so an 11-mile day was planned. There was nothing there to suggest it turning into a 15-mile day that would include perhaps the most dangerous one hour of hiking on the entire trail. As we hiked to the summit of West Peak Baldpate Mountain, the rain picked up, as did the wind thus lowering the temperature. Within five minutes Tom and I realized nothing good was going to happen on this large treeless piece of unforgiving rock. At that point, the smart thing to do would have been to retreat. It never entered my mind, full speed ahead was the mantra of the hiking world and the east peak was yet left to traverse. The wind picked up even more to the point of altering the way we walked; it was head down and leaning into the wind. Numerous times I was blown sideways only for the wind to stop causing me to then almost fall over. It was a tough walk, our rain gear was no match for the wind driven rain but once below tree line the wind stopped and Frye Notch Lean-to was only a couple miles away. Five other hikers at the shelter greeted us and even though it was early afternoon most were tucked into their sleeping bags and planning to stay there until the weather broke. I was wet from head to toe but I had dry clothing in my pack. One of the hikers happened to be a young lady, causing me to make an announcement, "Young lady" I stated, "I'm about to get extremely naked here so I would appreciate your consideration." She laughed as did everyone else, "Go for it," she said, "I've been putting up with this stuff for the past five months." The warmth returned to my body quickly and rather than spend the night at what would have been a crowded shelter the decision was made to march on four more miles where a shuttle would take us into Andover and a hostel called The Cabin.

Tom made one phone call and it turned into magic, the shuttle driver and owner of the hostel was at the road waiting for us, almost unheard of on the A.T. And this, upon pulling into the Cabin, Earl told us, "If you guys need to go into town the keys to the truck are in the ashtray," I do not know if this is common practice or if he just makes an allowance for old helpless guys like Tom and myself. Earl and wife Margie along with son Don were in their 18th year of running the Cabin. Margie is a great cook and makes every effort to impress while preparing an evening meal that is not only scrumptious but also easy on the pocket book. The Cabin and the people running it are icons of the trail.

A plan with Don was worked out for the next day to shuttle us back to the trailhead then hike ten miles and be picked up again and driven back to the Cabin where another night could be spent under a roof with four walls.

The trail maintenance volunteers make our hiking possible while the hostel owners and shuttle drivers make it so much easier.

We also had a mail drop at the post office in Andover, as it would take about four and a half days of food before re-supplying again 60 miles up the trail in Stratton. The five-day forecast called for almost perfect hiking weather. Autumn was upon us and the nights did get a little cold but nothing extreme. I continued picking blueberries, mostly at elevations over 2,000 feet. My appetite for Cliff Bars, dehydrated Mountain House meals and oatmeal is beginning to wane so I am relying on candy bars and trail mix to keep my energy levels up. My consumption of ibuprofen ran between 800 and 1,200 mg a day. Probably not a good thing to do but so goes my hike to Katahdin. I accepted help where I could get it and I was eating constantly to maintain my weight so it did not upset my stomach. As I look to the north, it appears the mountains are less jagged, gentler, less imposing ascents to the summit and descents on the other side. One particular day there were no climbs over 500 feet. There are ten or 12 of us moving together as a loosely knit community. Most are genuine through hikers, class of 2011. Some started in early March, some have been together from Springer Mt. Tom and I are the only section hikers in the group but they treat us like family. Once in Stratton, Mt. Katahdin will be only 188 miles away and I have yet to see a moose although I have walked through a boxcar of droppings. The days turned exceptionally warm, cooling off little at night forcing me to sleep on top of my sleeping bag.

The last day before Stratton required only an eight-mile hike to Maine 27 and a short hitch into town. Tom called ahead to make reservations at the White Wolf Inn. As luck would have it, they are closed on Tuesdays but the woman said she would leave a key in the door of room seven. You just have to love small towns and the people that call them home. Once showered and laundry done it was a short walk across the street to Fotter's Market where I purchased a large deli sandwich, a container of potato salad, two quarts of chocolate milk, 20 ounce bottle of vitamin water, and a 12 ounce can of Diet Coke. I carried this back to the room and ate it all. I was hoping to buy another gas canister for my cook stove but one was not to be found in this town. Now I would worry about making it to our next re-supply in Munson.

Back on the trail Wednesday morning at 8 A.M. and eight miles later we stood on the summit of 4,145-foot Bigelow Mountain. It is the last climb over 4,000 feet until reaching Katahdin. Tom visited with a couple day hikers from New York that were out climbing the 4,000-foot mountains in the Northeast. I believe there are 150 of them and they had only three remaining. It is a project they started in 1980. I guess everyone has his or her own Katahdin, or an Albatross hanging around their neck. Right now, all I have is a toenail coming off and it hurts every time I put my foot down. I may have to increase my allocation of Ibuprofen if it continues. The word on the trail today is not good, due to Hurricane Irene the trail in Vermont is closed for the season.

Chasing the white blazes the first day out of Stratton came slowly as less than 11 miles were covered and it still required a great deal of work. We have made a decision to take a zero in Monson, our bodies are screaming for a day off and being this close to Katahdin it would be foolish to risk an overuse injury.

The second day was not much better, only 12 miles in the log book. Camp that night was at West Carry Pond Lean-to. A 67-year-old retired Navy guy also spent the night. He was a submariner and served during the transition time between diesel and nuclear powered boats. He told us some interesting stories;

167

passing the hour before hiker mid-night very quickly.

The third day out of Stratton came the Kennebec River, a river so wide, so intimidating that the official Appalachian Trail requires a canoe ride across it. Every day from 9-11 a.m. and 2-4 p.m., a Registered Maine Master Guide shows up with a canoe and ferries hikers two at a time across the mighty river. Signed release forms and life jackets for the 10-minute ride were mandatory. The guide told us to expect freezing temperatures tonight but it did not materialize. It may have dropped to about 40 degrees but no colder.

Sunday morning, September 18, our camp is 14 miles out of Monson and we enthusiastically want to be there sooner rather than later. The trail was mostly a gentle downhill to Maine 15. It was an easy hitch for a three-mile ride into town. Our last mail drops will be waiting for us at the post office, mostly dehydrated Mountain House meals. Previously I have not been to this town and all I know about it is what I read in the guidebook but I just know I am going to like it; I very much need a day off. Tom, myself, and several others stayed at the Lake Shore House, 55 bucks a night, worth every penny of it. We also filled a five-gallon bucket with food to be delivered, for 15 dollars, approximately 30 miles up the trail at a road crossing so the march out of Monson will be with light food bags. It was a very relaxing day off the trail, eating restaurant food, doing laundry and making plans for the last 114 miles of the hike. This time of the year in this part of the country the weather seems to be unpredictable so at best all a person can do is hope it stays half way decent. Before leaving Monson on Tuesday morning, I considered taking one more shower but talked myself out of it in favor of wanting to smell like a real long distance hiker when I reached the summit of Katahdin.

After racking up 15 miles the first day; most likely on adrenalin alone as everyone was fired-up knowing that in seven days the end of this trail would be ours. The lean-to at Long Pond Stream would serve as camp that night. The temperature dropped a good deal during the early morning hours forcing me to sleep with my rain gear on. At 6:00 that morning Tom and I were up and making breakfast trying to be as quiet as possible as to not disturb other hikers in the lean-to. It seldom works that way, generally if one person gets up it is impossible for anyone to stay sleeping. Us older guys are the ones hiking at 6:30 am and it is the younger ones sleeping until nine. In my haste to keep the noise to a minimum, I left behind my dry clothes bag and a pair of wet dirty socks. They would be repatriated almost 15 miles down the trail as Rain Gear; almost certain it was my stuff presented them to me as I sat on side of the trail having a bite to eat. Most other hikers would have done the same with the dry clothes bag but to pick up another hikers dirty socks and transport them for the better part of the day is unbelievable. Thank you again Rain Gear.

The trail now runs through the 100-mile wilderness area that is very remote but not really a wilderness area as there is an occasional road crossing. It was encouraging when looking at the maps through this area that only two climbs of any degree were

169

ahead of us. Many small up's and down's were encountered along with a good deal of bog. At times, it was deep bog; one misplaced foot could result in sinking in the mud well past the knee. Also there were several rivers to ford. Very cold rivers, if done in the morning it would wake you up faster than a cup of hot Folgers. Because of the thick fog hanging in the air, we missed at least three opportunities to see Katahdin from a distance. The first view of our destination would come while standing on Abol Bridge, just 10 trail miles from the base of the mountain.

The atmosphere on the trail was jovial. The end was in sight, the end of the trail for all and the through hikers the end of a way of life. I am quite sure I will not forget my five years out here but I am positive they will always remember their five of six months. They have few peers and I congratulate them. Every state gives you the best it has to offer and the worst it has to offer, an accumulation of the two and you have the trail. This endeavor is littered with many excuses and opportunities to walk away, return home, live a more conventional life, a much easier life but somehow a few, a very few have the courage and stamina to stick it out until the very end.

When asked why he wanted to climb Mt. Everest, George Mallory stated, "Because it's there." I do not know if that is a good reason to hike this trail. I am sure everyone out here has a reason but for most, it is for the love of hiking.

At noon on Thursday I reached the 2,530 summit of White Cap Mountain, Katahdin lay 73 trail miles to the north. I picked small almost tasteless blueberries, they would be the last. The climbing is over; the rest of the trail consists of small hills and more bog. Cedar swamps so thick the sun never reaches the forest floor. Exposed tree roots, always slippery, always waiting to claim another victim. The going is slow but inclement weather is on its way. We tented at the East Branch Lean-to, 63 miles from Katahdin Stream Campground which will be our final camping place before climbing the big mountain.

Baxter State Park, home to Katahdin posts daily weather reports during the hiking season with only a "Class 1" report allowing hiking above tree line. At this time of year, it is not uncommon for rain to move in and completely halt climbing where the trees no longer grow. Word was moving fast on the trail that Monday would be the last good climbing day with Tuesday becoming doubtful. Myself, Tom, and maybe six others decided to hike the next 63 miles in three days. Unfortunately, the first 20 would be in the rain, making the trail a muddy mess and the rivers a little more challenging to ford. This was the breaking point for my feet, until now, with great care, I had few problems with them but this day they remained wet and I developed several blisters on my toes. It was a demanding three days but we made it. Our grinding march turned out to be unnecessary as the inclement weather held off until later in the week. My first look at Katahdin came on Sunday around noon. The Abol Bridge spans the West Branch of the Penobscot River and offers a fantastic view of Katahdin. Still a good nine trail miles from the mountain she stands there with all the dignity and grandiose a person would expect after hiking almost 2,200 miles. From the bridge, it looks like she is there alone with no smaller mountains on her flanks. Like all the rocks in the state of Maine were used to make just this one mountain but this is deceiving and I would soon find that she has friends, lesser in stature but no less magnificent to view, particularly from the summit of Katahdin.

After several pictures, none that did the mountain justice I strolled over to Linda's Store at Abol Bridge for a deli sandwich, a Diet Coke, and a can of sardines. I do not know why I bought the fish but they tasted all right. Along with eight other hikers, we shared a picnic table that has no doubt been used by hundreds of hikers with a sense of achievement setting in. For the most part the big walk was over having only a nine mile hike to Katahdin Stream Campground where most of us would pitch our tents for the last time. I ate just about everything in my food bag, saving only special items for tomorrows climb. Hiker midnight came early, at 7:30 I found myself zipped into my tent looking for sleep that I would not easily find. This was the end, no more sleeping in this tent, on this air mattress that has served me so well. I ate a candy bar about 8:30 and at midnight, the real midnight; I was spreading peanut butter and honey on a whole-wheat soft taco. The next morning Tom confessed he also slept little. Sixty-two year old men so excited sleep does not come easy. Can it get any better?

The tent site rests at about 1,250 feet and in the

course of five miles we would climb to 5,267 feet, it started easy, turned easier said than done, turned very difficult, got relatively easy on the Tableland and adrenaline carried us to the top. We were greeted by eight or ten other hikers already on the summit. I noticed a champagne bottle, I was offered a can of beer, which I refused thinking of the hike down, and the smell of a left handed lucky filled the air. Everyone was in high spirits, a few were happy and sad and I think we were all relieved. Pictures were taken standing in front of, behind, and on top of the plywood sign designating the summit of Katahdin.

I believe this mountain plays a secondary role to the better-known Mt Rainier in stature but I think no mountaineer has ever felt as triumphant standing on the summit of Rainier as I did that morning on Katahdin.

I broke out my cook stove to boil water for coffee and Tom opened a ham and egg Mountain House breakfast. One last meal sitting on a rock was only fitting.

The hike down was slow and savored but uneventful. We stopped to exchange congratulations with Boy Scout, Rain Gear, and his father as they approached the summit.

Once back at the campground several of us waited an hour for the shuttle into Millinocket where everyone booked a bunk at the Appalachian Trail Lodge for 25 bucks, took showers, washed clothes, and of course ate restaurant food. It never tasted so good. Our wives picked us up the next day; it was back to the world.

As for that old guy telling me he was going to sell his gear and buy a bowling ball, that was me.

AFTER WORD

Now that I am done with the trail I do not miss it. It 's doubtful I would ever do the whole trail again but what I do miss is the camaraderie that develops between hikers from all over the world. Some I knew only in passing, others for a few days and some I still have contact with via e-mail.

I guess luck played a part in that no serious illness or injuries occurred from the falls we took. It is a long trail, your body has many opportunities to break down, and every step increases the chance for a ticket off the trail. Everyone donates a little blood to the trail, it is expected and accepted and a little blood running down your leg as you walk into a campsite only makes for good conversation.

I cannot tell you how difficult this trail is, only those that choose to hike it can know. As T. S. Elliot proclaimed, "Only those who will risk going too far can possibly find out how far one can go." I planned to do this alone but putting everything in prospective I have to thank Tom for making it possible.

So that is my account of hiking the Appalachian Trail. I hope you enjoyed it.

Buck Innerebner lives five miles from his childhood home in the Upper Peninsula of Michigan with his wife of 44 years.

Repd@bellsouth.net

CPSIA information can be obtained at www.ICGtesting.com
Printed in the USA
LVOW01s1947060214

372657LV00032B/1654/P

9 781469 904269